CHURCHES IN CHARLESTON

Dissenter
1. Circular Congregational Church
2. French Huguenot Church
3. Quaker Cemetery Fence

Episcopal
4. St. Philip's Episcopal Church
5. St. Michael's Episcopal Church
6. Cathedral of St. Luke and St. Paul
7. St. Stephen's Episcopal Church
8. Grace Episcopal Church
9. Church of the Holy Communion
10. St. Mark's Episcopal Church

Baptist
11. First Baptist Church
12. Citadel Square Baptist Church
13. New Tabernacle Fourth Baptist Church
14. Central Baptist Church

Presbyterian
15. First (Scots) Presbyterian Church
16. Second Presbyterian Church

Lutheran
17. St. John's Lutheran Church
18. St. Andrew's Lutheran Church
19. St. Johannes Lutheran Church
20. St. Matthew's Lutheran Church

Jewish
21. Kahal Kadosh Beth Elohim
22. Brith Sholom Beth Israel

Roman Catholic
23. St. Mary's Catholic Church
24. Cathedral of St. John the Baptist
25. St. Patrick's Catholic Church

Methodist
26. Trinity United Methodist Church
27. Bethel United Methodist Church
28. St. James United Methodist Church
29. Old Bethel United Methodist Church
30. Centenary United Methodist Church

African Methodist Episcopal
31. Emanuel A.M.E. Church
32. Morris Brown A.M.E. Church
33. Mt. Zion A.M.E. Church

Unitarian-Universalist
34. Unitarian Church

Reformed Episcopal
35. Holy Trinity Reformed Episcopal Church
36. St. John's Reformed Episcopal Church

Interdenominational
37. St. Luke's Chapel, MUSC

Greek Orthodox
38. Holy Trinity Greek Orthodox Church

The Churches of Charleston and the Lowcountry

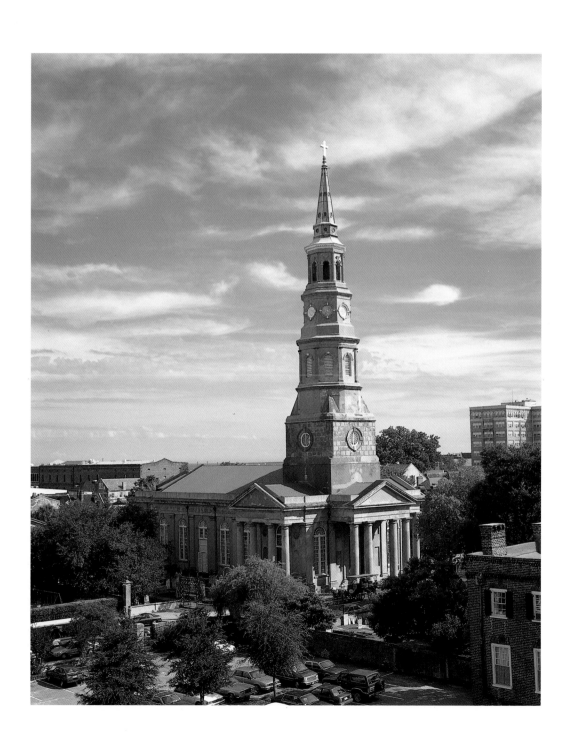

*A*bove: Circular Congregational Church

*O*verleaf: St. Philip's Episcopal on Church Street, the oldest church organization in Charleston

*O*pposite: Old St. Andrew's Episcopal Church, on S.C. Highway 61 west of Charleston

The Churches of Charleston and the Lowcountry

The Preservation Society of Charleston

Introduction by George C. Rogers, Jr.

Photographs by Ron Anton Rocz

Edited by Mary Moore Jacoby

University of South Carolina Press

To the memory of Samuel Gaillard Stoney

—⋗◦⋖—

Copyright © 1994 The Preservation Society of Charleston

Published in Columbia, South Carolina, by the
University of South Carolina Press

Manufactured in Hong Kong

LIBRARY OF CONGRESS CATALOGING-IN-PUBLICATION DATA

The churches of Charleston and the lowcountry / Preservation Society
    of Charleston; with an introduction by George C. Rogers, Jr.;
    photographs by Ron Anton Rocz; edited by Mary Moore Jacoby.
        p.   cm.
    Includes bibliographical references and index.
    ISBN 0-87249-888-3 (acid-free)
1. Church architecture—South Carolina—Charleston. 2. Church
architecture—South Carolina. 3. Charleston (S.C.)—Buildings, structures, etc.   I. Jacoby, Mary Moore.   II. Preservation Society
of Charleston.
NA5235.C37C58 1993
726'.5'09757915—dc20   93-10057
                                                   CIP

Curved pews, Circular Congregational Church

———◦———

Therefore, any Seven or more Persons agreeing in any Religion, shall constitute a Church or Profession, to which they shall give Some name, to distinguish it from others. . . . No Man of any other Church or Profession shall disturb or molest any Religious Assembly. . . . It shall be lawful for Slaves as all others, to enter them selves, and be of what Church or Profession any of them shall think best, and thereof be as fully Members as any Freeman. . . . No Person whatsoever, shall disturb, molest or persecute another for his speculative Opinions in Religion, or his way of Worship.

The Fundamental Constitutions of Carolina,
the First Day of March, 1669

T*he French Huguenot Church is the earliest example of*
Gothic Revival architecture found in Charleston.

Contents

Foreword

On behalf of the members of the Preservation Society of Charleston, we are pleased to offer this book on Charleston's religious heritage. We believe it fills a long-standing need for an updated survey of churches in and near Charleston since the work of Mr. Lilly and Mr. Legerton has been so long out of print. For us, the publication of this book represents another aspect of preservation progress as the Society, in its 73rd year, continues to move forward to accomplish its purpose of encouraging interest in the preservation of structures of historic or aesthetic significance. We believe that this publication can help us to achieve our goal of preventing the destruction or defacement of such buildings as are described in the following pages because the information presented reinforces their importance both locally and nationally.

Certainly the Preservation Society was put to the test in this regard after the devastation of Hurricane Hugo in September 1989. The storm damaged virtually every church in the city. Some, such as St. Luke's Chapel, were nearly destroyed. Others, such as the Second Presbyterian Church, St. John's Lutheran Church, and the Cathedral of St. Luke and St. Paul, were so badly damaged that only the strength of will and the commitment of caring congregations brought these churches back into active use. Throughout the recovery process the Preservation Society has worked with these groups to offer assistance, advice, and support.

Today, the work of restoring St. Luke's Chapel has begun. This effort is perhaps the most telling evidence of an attitude of caring that has characterized this city since its inception. Once again, the city motto, "She guards her customs, her buildings and her laws," has been realized as Charlestonians responded to this natural disaster with energy and determination. The photographs on the following pages document the value we place as an organization on the authenticity of the restoration efforts, the diversity of the architecture, and the integrity of the craftsmanship.

The Preservation Society is indebted to the many congregations who opened their places of worship to the photographer for this book. Special thanks go to our editor, Mary Moore Jacoby, who saw the publication to completion and still managed daily tasks as director of the Preservation Resource Center.

John Meffert, Executive Director
The Preservation Society of Charleston
Charleston, South Carolina

The sanctuary of Charleston's Central
Baptist Church. The wall and ceiling murals
were painted by an itinerant artist.

A *church building casts its influence upon a community for years, sometimes for generations. A noble building seems to have an almost living air and spirit, and may become a benign power in the lives of the people round about it. It is a great blessing, to any town to possess such a structure.*

Van Ogden Vogt

Preface

Charleston is one of the principal settings for the advance of religious freedom in America. Through a lengthy evolution that began as early as 1680, divergent groups of varied religious persuasions settled in Charleston and the surrounding countryside. This emerging city in the New World became a host to religious liberty, serving as an early forum for the separation of Church and State through the disestablishment of the Church as a tax-supported civil authority. Charleston helped fashion this principle into the nation's founding constitutional mandate, sending her best representatives to advocate religious liberty for a new government by the people.

This is a story not as widely known as it should be. But the extraordinary diversity of historical religious structures in the old city of Charleston and its surroundings stands as monumental testimony that all are entitled to freedom of assembly, freedom of speech, and freedom of religion.

Seven years ago our photographer, Ron Anton Rocz, began his mammoth project of a photographic survey of the historic religious buildings in and around Charleston. After the 1989 hurricane he returned to many of these sacred places to document their destruction and later their rejuvenation. He viewed these churches and synagogues as an "inner landscape" of incredible beauty, rarely seen in its entirety by any single individual, and as historical architecture of social importance.

We at the Preservation Society of Charleston are fortunate that Mr. Rocz chose to bring his work to our publications committee to ask for our help in writing and publishing a book focusing on Charleston's religious architecture as a vital element in the social history of the city. Our board

agreed that the history of these structures is a story worthy of recognition, a reflection of the ethnic and social history of the city. The project also fit our own preservation mission. As these buildings have survived wars, fires, earthquake, and storms of both natural and theological derivation, they have in turn survived the bulldozer and economic hardships. Their duration is something dear to the hearts of preservationists, no matter what our religious orientation. No matter what progression of events we favor, these buildings endure as evidence of the resilience of the human spirit. We see the book as a tribute to that spirit.

In the process of organizing the book, we decided to arrange it by denomination and date of origination of the congregation rather than by the date of any given structure. Many churches have been rebuilt several times, have been moved to other locations, or have housed more than one congregation. We determined that we should organize the chronology in a way that would help to describe when the various religious groups came to Charleston. (A table in the back of the book lists the chronology of dates of origin and of present structures.)

With a few exceptions we have concentrated on existing buildings constructed before 1900 that have not undergone regrettable alteration.

Photographs were made both before and after Hurricane Hugo in 1989. The effort was made to rephotograph when the restoration of a church was significant, as it was at Citadel Square Baptist when the original steeple was reproduced. In some cases, restoration is still under way as we proceed to publication.

—*Mary Moore Jacoby, Editor*

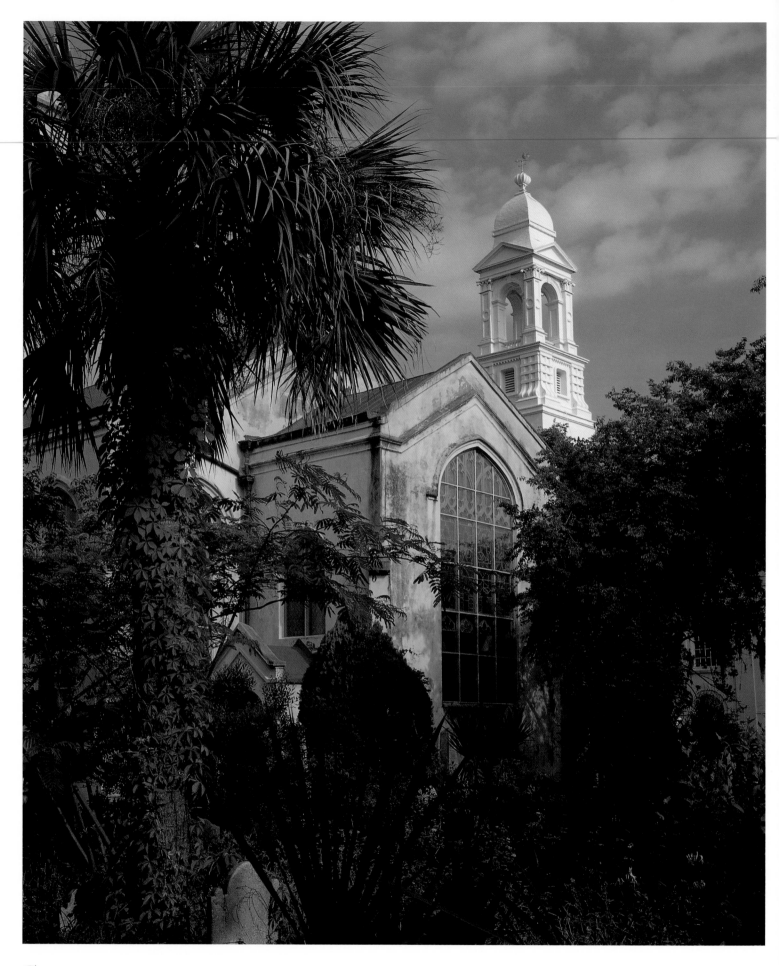

*C*hurches Of Charleston : the Unitarian Church and behind it the steeple of St John's Lutheran Church

Acknowledgments

Through their support, cooperation, and assistance the publications committee and the board of the Preservation Society of Charleston have been responsible for making this book a reality. Frances Tindall deserves special recognition for giving editorial direction, lending her publishing experience, and hosting a writing retreat at her Edisto Island residence. Mary Dean Richards, Kyra Kuhar, Michael McLaughlin, Joan Algar, and Charles W. Watson worked especially hard for this book.

We are grateful to Dr. George C. Rogers, Jr., for his expertise in writing the introduction and to the Reverend A. Coile Estes for sharing her discussion of church preservation and stewardship for our conclusion.

Sally Reahard, a life member of the Society since 1975, contributed financially to our endeavor. Elias Bull provided consultation and research on some of the lesser-known churches. Warren Slesinger at the University of South Carolina Press was diligent in his effort to bring our book to publication. Lynn Meffert proofread and indexed the book. Ann Goold gave needed polish while typing the manuscript. David B. McCormack and Robert H. Mozingo provided legal counsel. Sarah Fick of Preservation Consultants helped to verify dates and other information. Ron Rocz and John Coles designed the location maps. Mary Koonts and Julie Rowe, preservation interns, assisted with book preparation and information gathering.

Cindy Clark, Maria Curtiss, Bryan L. Finch, Yvette Richardson Guy, the Reverend

St. Thomas and St. Denis Episcopal Church Cemetery

Monsignor Lawrence B. McInerny, the Reverend Robert L. Oliveros, Ron Anton Rocz, Frances Tindall, Charles W. Watson, Kristi Sanders, and Keith L. Compton made noteworthy contributions to the text through research and writing. Our readers were Elise Pinckney, George C. Rogers, Jr., Jean Badger Lynn, Frances Tindall, Mary Koonts, and Spencer Tolley.

Special thanks go to those who responded to our call for updated, condensed histories of the churches and synagogues. We were encouraged by the number of historians, pastors, and interested individuals who came forward.

The following people provided help or sent

us church histories: the Reverend George J. Tompkins of Old St. Andrew's, Charlotte Hay, the Reverend Barry D. Van Deventer, and Jack Thomson of First Scots, Sister Anne Francis Campbell and the Reverend Monsignor Sam R. Miglarese of the Cathedral of St. John the Baptist, the Reverend Albert H. Keller of Circular Congregational Church, Felder Hutchinson of St. Mark's, the Reverend Richard I. H. Belser of St. Michael's, Ann Fripp Hampton of St. Paul's, John Slayton of St. Thomas and St. Denis, Martha La Rue Riebe and the Reverend Philip C. Bryant of the French Huguenot Church, Louisa M. Montgomery of the Cathedral of St. Luke and St. Paul, Solomon Breibart and Rabbi William A. Rosenthal of Beth Elohim, John H. Boineau of Christ St. Paul's Church, the Reverend Joseph L. O'Brien of St. Patrick's, William David Redd of First Baptist, Audrey M. Hill of St. Andrew's Lutheran, Agatha Aimar Simmons and Florence Marie Hennessy of St. Mary's, Harriet G. Simpson of Mt. Zion A.M.E., Deacon J. A. Wigfall of Central Baptist, Ernie Tunnell and Doris Meadowcroft of Grace Episcopal, Julia Hills of Johns Island Presbyterian, the Reverend Walter G. Cook of Second Presbyterian, Annie Jenkins Batson of Rockville Presbyterian, the Reverend James Lowry of Mount Pleasant Presbyterian, Joseph Holleman and the Reverend Edward L. Moore of Summerville Presbyterian, Dr. J. Ronald Moock of Cummins Memorial Theological Seminary, John E. Gibbs of Pompion Hill, Ann Andrus of Bethel, the Reverend Boyce F. Brooks of Centenary, the Reverend Walk Jones of the Presbyterian Church on Edisto, and Elias Bull. We have also drawn from Robert Stockton's past newspaper accounts on the architecture and history of many of the buildings.

Left: New Tabernacle Fourth Baptist Church, originally St. Luke's Episcopal Church

Opposite: Christ Episcopal Church bell tower, Mount Pleasant

The Churches of Charleston and the Lowcountry

T*he sanctuary of Charleston's Grace Episcopal Church*

Introduction

by George C. Rogers, Jr.

The climate of religious autonomy that promoted the organization of so many early churches in Charleston was fostered by forces at work in Europe as the city evolved. It would be inaccurate to think of Charleston as a completely Anglican enclave. Though the Anglican Church was established in 1706, the dissenting elements were strong in the city. The Dissenters were those who would not accept the Anglican settlement made for the Church of England after the restoration of Charles II in 1660. Prominent among the first immigrants were the French Huguenots. The history of their escape from France, both before and after the Revocation of the Edict of Nantes in 1685, was in the revolutionary tradition that was characteristic of all the national groups that contributed to the founding of Charleston.

There was the perennial question of unity versus diversity that wracked Western Europe after the oneness of its Christianity had been undermined by the writings and teachings of Martin Luther and John Calvin. These leaders of the Reformation did not object to unity. They simply wanted to purify the Church, not destroy it. In England, Henry VIII had been the original architect of the Church of England. The episcopal hierarchy was maintained with the Archbishop of Canterbury replacing the Pope in Rome. The Book of Common Prayer, the glory of the Reformation in England, replaced the Latin liturgy with an English liturgy. In the sixteenth century under the Tudors, the state religion depended upon who was head of

The sanctuary of Mount Pleasant Presbyterian Church, with balconies reopened after the renovation and enlargement completed in 1982

the Church. Mary Tudor was Catholic; Elizabeth Tudor was Protestant. When in 1603 James IV of Scotland became James I of England, the great question was what form the Church should take. The failure of Queen Mary to win her subjects back to Catholicism and the defeat of the Spanish Armada in 1588 meant that the theological settlement would have to be a Protestant one.

In Scotland, John Knox achieved a Presbyterian settlement that might have served the King, but the King wished to include all Protestant groups. There were those who wanted to further purify the Church of England, calling for each congregation to select its own minister. But this congregationalism implied a very loose-knit national church with each congregation more or less autonomous. There were those who wanted to go still further and as a group were called Separatists. The most famous of these were the Pilgrims who journeyed to Plymouth; the most influential ultimately were the Baptists. If each congregation had been left to go its own way, there might have been peace and quiet within the kingdom, but Charles I and Archbishop Laud were determined to move in the direction of Rome. For their obstinance they both lost their heads, Archbishop Laud in 1645 and Charles I in 1649.

There ensued the English Civil War (1640–1660), sometimes called the Puritan Revolution. There were two phases. The first pitted the English Presbyterians, supported by the Scots and the Congregationalists (the Independents), behind their leader, Oliver Cromwell, against the King. After curtailing the powers of the Crown and the Church, however, they fell out with each other. The second phase ended with the triumph of Oliver Cromwell and his New Model Army. The Cromwellian Interregnum, with the Independents in control, lasted a decade.

There were economic forces also at work. English gentry, who grew rich from the confiscation of Church properties, were willing to support a king if the King would listen to them in their parliament and respect their rights as Englishmen. This was the group that eventually decided that contest in favor of the recall of Charles II in 1660 and the establishment of the Church of England along Anglican lines. Those ministers who refused to use the Book of Common Prayer and to acknowledge the power of the bishops were excluded from their parishes. Many of these then continued the migration to New England, founded before the first phase of the Revolution in England. In 1660, the Church of Scotland was organized and bishops and the Covenantors persecuted.

Many country gentry who had supported Charles II were created baronets in the early 1660s, but the greatest reward went in 1665 to eight individuals who received the enormous grant of Carolina, an area that stretched from Virginia to Florida. When the eight Lords Proprietors, led by Lord Ashley and his secretary, John Locke, drew up the Fundamental Constitutions for their new property, they envisioned a refuge for those who had been in dissent against the 1660 religious settlement. According to the Fundamental Constitutions of 1669, "any Seven or more Persons agreeing in any Religion, shall constitute a Church or Profession, to which they shall give Some name, to distinguish it from others." There were three prerequisites to which the members must agree. "That there is a God. That God is publicly to be worshiped. That it is lawful, and the duty of every man, being thereunto called by those that Govern, to bear witness to truth; and that every church or profession shall, in their Terms of Communion, Set down the external way whereby they witness a truth as in the presence of God, whether it be by laying hands on and Kissing the Gospel, as in the Protestant and Papist Churches, or by holding up the hand, or any other Sensible way."

The first fleet in 1670 brought Barbadians, who were followers of the Church of England. Then in 1680 came the French Huguenots, and in 1684 the Scottish Covenantors. The original Anglican parish was that of St. Philip's, a church being erected on the southeast corner of Meeting and Broad Streets.

The Independent or Congregational Church established in Charleston prior to 1690 was the mother church of the Dissenters who settled in Carolina. This group, composed of Presbyterians from Scotland and Ireland, Congregationalists from Old and New England, and French Huguenots, built its White Meeting House on the street that bears its name. The Huguenots built their own church in 1687 on the southeast corner of Dock (now Queen) Street and Church Street.

Two other dissenting groups, the Baptists and the Quakers, were present almost from the beginning. The Baptists had a structure on

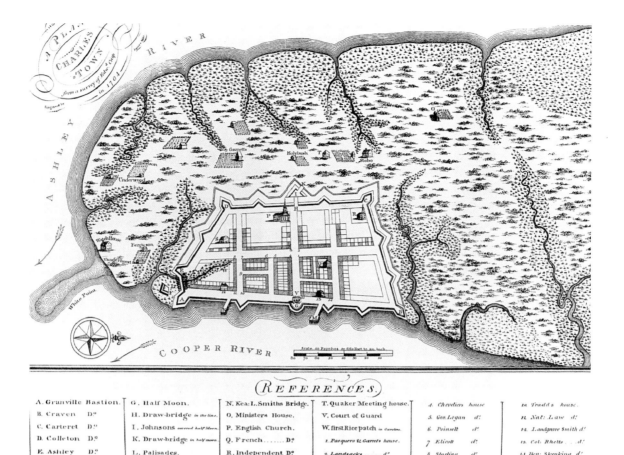

A PLAN of CHARLES TOWN from a survey of Rob.t Crisp in 1704

ASHLEY RIVER

COOPER RIVER

White Point

Scale 40 Perches or 660 feet to an inch

REFERENCES.

A. Granville Bastion.	G. Half Moon.	N. Kea: L. Smiths Bridge.	T. Quaker Meeting house.
B. Craven D.º	H. Draw-bridge *in the line.*	O. Ministers House.	V. Court of Guard
C. Carteret D.º	I. Johnsons *covered half Moon.*	P. English Church.	W. first Rice patch *in Carolina.*
D. Colleton D.º	K. Draw-bridge *in half moon.*	Q. French ...... D.º	1. *Pasquero & Garrets house.*
E. Ashley D.º	L. Palisades.	R. Independent D.º	2. *Landsacks .... d.º*
F. Blakes D.º	M. L.t Col. Rhetts Bridge.	S. Ana baptist D.º	3. *Jn.º Croskeys ..... d.º*

4. *Chevaliers house*	10. *Tradds house.*
5. *Geo. Logan d.º*	11. *Nat: Law d.º*
6. *Poinsett d.º*	12. *Landgrave Smith d.º*
7. *Elicott d.º*	13. *Col: Rhetts ... d.º*
8. *Starling d.º*	14. *Hen: Skenking d.º*
9. *M.t Boone d.º*	15. *Sindery ...... d.º*

Map by Edward Crisp from a 1704 survey

lower Church Street, and the Quaker Meeting House was on King Street. Edward Crisp's 1704 map, the first religious map of Charleston, identified these churches along with the first St. Philip's. The Presbyterians broke away from the Meeting Street congregation in 1731 and founded the First Scots Church on the southwest corner of Tradd and Meeting Streets. The Lutherans organized St. John's Lutheran Church around 1742. The Jewish population, in Charleston since 1695, organized Beth Elohim in 1749.

Around 1700, a great undertaking was under way in England to bring all Protestant denominations within the forms and under the hierarchy of the Church of England. The Society for the Promotion of Christian Knowledge (1698) and the Society for the Propagation of the Gospel in Foreign Parts (1701) provided funds for the establishment of libraries and of missionaries. In Charleston, Chief Justice Nicholas Trott in the realm of the law, Governor

Sir Nathaniel Johnson in the area of politics, and Commissary Gideon Johnston in the sphere of religion worked together to establish the Church of England in the province. There was never a bishop in the colonies as all colonials came under the authority of the Bishop of London. The Bishop of London did from time to time appoint a commissary who would exercise all the functions of a bishop except for ordination and confirmation.

In the Church Act of 1706, the colony's settled area was divided into ten parishes, the parish church becoming the center of local culture. To accommodate the French Huguenots, two parishes, St. James Santee and St. Denis, were set aside for Anglican services using a Book of Common Prayer in French designed for England's Channel Islands. The Huguenot Church in Charleston, however, began using a liturgy developed in Neuchâtel, Switzerland, in 1555.

The work of the commissaries Gideon

Johnston (1707–1716), William Treadwell Bull (until 1723), and Alexander Garden (until 1756) was intended as a civilizing and culture-building force. The First Great Awakening, which began in 1740, created tensions between Alexander Garden, the commissary, and George Whitefield, the evangelical minister. There was always a need to strike a balance between authority and fragmentation.

Of equal importance was the movement to carry Christianity to the Native Americans and the African slaves. Both Indians and blacks were enslaved. The crucial question that had to be decided early on was whether baptized slaves would by dint of baptism become free persons. William Fleetwood, Bishop of St. Asaph in Wales, delivered a sermon in 1711 before the Society for the Propagation of the Gospel in Foreign Parts in which he implied that whether baptized or not, slaves remained slaves. He did emphasize, however, that the black man was not inferior to the white man, both being "equally the Workmanship of God." But the Church of England, whether it was led in the colony by Garden or by Whitefield, was determined to keep the slaves within the Church. The Negro Act of 1740, in force in South Carolina until the Civil War, described the spheres of the two races. Presumably, the Negro Act was to have been balanced by an experiment in the 1740s to educate the slaves, a concept initiated by Commissary Garden but not carried forward by his successors.

While the Church struggled to assert its authority, there was a provincial society forming in South Carolina. The Revolution of 1719 marked a break between the proprietary society of Lords Proprietors, Landgraves, and Cassiques and another set of classes—planters, merchants, and professional men—who were all growing rich from the profits obtained from the new staples of rice and indigo. The elite was quite willing to use its wealth to manifest its aspirations in churches and public buildings, notable examples being St. Michael's Church and the First State House.

The established church had public funds for building church structures. The eighteenth-century Anglican churches would never have been so magnificent if public resources had not been available. Not only were the ten parishes provided with parish churches, from the smallest, St. Andrew's, to the largest, St. Helena's, but when the first St. Philip's burned, it could be rebuilt in the 1720s with a soaring steeple and commodious space for its congregation. The second St. Philip's was given a more prominent location, the highest spot in town, placed almost in the center of the road, henceforth called Church Street.

In 1751 the parish of St. Philip's was divided into two parishes, St. Michael's below and St. Philip's above Broad Street. St. Michael's was intended to be more grand than St. Philip's. It was designed in the eighteenth-century high-fashion style that stemmed from Christopher Wren. The same law that funded the new church also funded the State House that stood where the Charleston County Courthouse stands today at the crossing of

Interior view of Charleston's First Baptist Church. Robert Mills, architect for the church, described the structure as "purely Greek in style, simply grand in its proportions, and beautiful in its detail."

Broad and Meeting Streets. St. Michael's Church and the State House were spectacular structures worthy of the newly enriched and continuously striving elite.

Numerous members of the Anglican Church in Charleston were willing to think in congregational terms and sent their sons to academies conducted by Dissenters in England. One Charlestonian wrote to his cousin, a Congregationalist minister in New England, "For my part I look on the difference [between the Anglicans and the Congregationalists as] of so little consequence that could I not conveniently communicate with the one I should with the Other." In 1740 the Dissenters were still over one-half of the population and always stronger in the city than in most of the Lowcountry parishes. De Brahm wrote in 1772 that, although the city was divided into two parishes, there were six meeting houses—an Independent, a Presbyterian, a French, a German, and two Baptist—as well as Quaker and Jewish assemblages. Although the congregations differed in religious principles and "in the knowledge of salvation," there was no disorder, for the city had been since its beginning "renound for concord, compleasance, courteousness, and tenderness towards each other, and more so towards foreigners, without regard or respect of nations or religion."

On the eve of the American Revolution the Anglican Church was in the ascendancy. The Whig elite, emerging from the Anglicans, the French Huguenots, and the Dissenters, was in favor of the established church, while the merchant members of the Scots Presbyterian Church provided the most numerous group of Loyalists.

Concessions to the various dissenting groups were necessary to maintain the unity of the patriot cause. These concessions occurred in two momentous steps taken during the years of the American Revolution. The first step was in 1778 when the Anglican Church was disestablished and the Protestant Church established in its place. The second step occurred in 1790 when all religious organizations were allowed to incorporate. The South Carolina society had thus moved from religious toleration in 1669 to religious freedom by 1791.

The Reverend William Tennent, a Congregationalist, was the driving force behind disestablishment, but he was ably assisted by David Ramsay (Congregationalist) and the Reverend Richard Furman (Baptist). The heart of the reform was to place all Protestant congregations on the same footing before the law. Each Protestant group could ask for an act of incorporation which would permit it to protect its property in a court of law.

It should be noted that the Anglican Church retained control of its buildings, glebe, and church-owned lands, even though the property had been purchased and sustained by funds from the public treasury. Some Dissenters argued that such property belonged to all the people and should be sold and the proceeds divided among all, but that course of action had very little chance of occurring. Unlike the case in Virginia where the question was contested in the courts of law, in South Carolina it was a fait accompli that no one tried to overturn. In essence that development acted as an early preservation movement.

The second Congregational Church, organized on Archdale Street in 1787, became the Unitarian Church in 1817. The Jews had a congregation at Beth Elohim from 1749, made up largely of Sephardic Jews who had arrived as early as 1695 from the Dutch settlements in the West Indies. Although at the time of the French Revolution one large group of French Catholics arrived from Santo Domingo, the Charleston Catholics were, on the whole, from Ireland, coming individually rather than in groups. The French and the Irish Catholics made up the original congregation of St. Mary's. The Jews and Catholics were on opposite sides of Hasell Street. Both congregations were incorporated on the same day in 1791.

With the establishment of the United States, it was necessary for American churches to come together in new national organizations.

As John Wesley stayed within the fold of the Anglican communion until his death in 1792, there was need for the Methodists to decide whether they wanted to remain within or to move outside the Church of England. The Methodists in the United States decided in 1783 and 1784 to create the Methodist Episcopal Church, building the Cumberland Street Church in 1786. The American Anglicans formed the Protestant Episcopal Church of the United States in 1790.

In the sixty years before the Civil War, there was an increasing multiplication of denominations and of churches. The revivals of 1802 and of 1833, sometimes described as the Second and Third Great Awakenings, sparked the expansion. This was the time of the churching of the people.

Robert Mills designed the most beautiful of the Greek Revival style churches on the site of the Reverend William Screven's church, the First Baptist Church. After the split of the Baptists in 1844 into Northern and Southern Conventions, the Baptists of the Southern Convention built Citadel Square Baptist Church in 1854.

The Methodists built Trinity in 1791 and Bethel in 1797. With the influx of the Germans and the Irish in the 1840s, St. John's, St. Johannes, and St. Matthew's were built for the Lutheran congregations, followed by the Cathedral of St. John the Baptist and St. Finbar and St. Patrick's for the Catholics.

The most important black congregation in antebellum Charleston was that of the African Methodist Episcopal church which was founded by Morris Brown in 1816 but which disappeared after the Denmark Vesey Insurrection of 1822. Between 1848 and 1849, Calvary Church was planned for a black congregation of Episcopalians and constructed on Beaufain Street. During these late antebellum years, black congregants were given the use of Trinity, St. James (Spring Street), and Old Bethel churches.

With the end of the Civil War and the freeing of the slaves, the number of black churches increased. The African Methodist Episcopal Church formed Emanuel and Mt. Zion on Calhoun Street, and later Morris Brown. After these were established, the most important addition to the black churches was the Episcopal church of St. Mark's. The attempt to maintain mixed congregations by those churches that had permitted blacks to use their galleries for services did not last. The records show that in 1866 and 1867, African Americans asked for letters of dismission from those churches and joined the black churches of their denominations. The bitterness engendered during the Reconstruction period would end with a segregated world of churches that, for the most part, still endures.

The diversity that was a principal and unique characteristic of the Charleston religious scene created an environment in which great houses of worship continue to be built in Charleston. Since the nineteenth century, congregations such as Holy Trinity Greek Orthodox Church have brought to the city their own remarkable culture and beauty. The churches photographed for this book are the visible remains of the struggles to transplant the Old World religions to the new land. To enter and to ponder the history of each structure left behind is to know the history of Charleston more intimately.

Liberty being the only sure and lasting Foundation of our Quiet and Satisfaction in this world, a Community can never be reduced to any State . . . it must necessarily be their common interest to preserve.

Daniel Defoe, The Case of Protestant Dissenters in Carolina, *1706*

ONE

Dissenter

The promise of religious liberty was a powerful enticement to those who chose to journey to colonial Charles Towne. While many sought freedom in the New England colonies, the prevailing laissez-faire outlook in early Charles Towne was decidedly more cosmopolitan than that found in the Puritan culture in the North. Charles Towne, unlike Boston and Philadelphia, was founded by the diversity of commerce rather than by any one religious movement.

Although the established Anglican Church was supported by public taxes, membership in it was not compulsory. Neither was the practice of another religion restricted by law, thanks to the provision for religious tolerance provided by Lord Anthony Ashley Cooper, Proprietor of Carolina, later the first Earl of Shaftesbury. Lord Ashley, with the help of John Locke, drafted the Fundamental Constitutions for Carolina affirming religious toleration. The Proprietors later revised Article 96 from a general declaration of tolerance into a more explicit statement with the Anglican Church as the established church. Their alteration to the document also called for church membership in some officially recognized religious organization but retained "liberty of conscience."

This model for the free practice of faith had great appeal for those early groups known as Dissenters in colonial Charles Towne—Huguenots, Anabaptists, Quakers, Presbyterians, and Congregationalists, followed by the Lutherans and the Jews. As the Anglican Church gave way to the issue of separation of

Church and State, the concept of religious liberty replaced that of "toleration." In his 1777 petition opposing a continued religious establishment in the drafting of a new constitution, Congregationalist minister William Tennent called for universal equality when he asked rhetorically, "How can a Dissenter enjoy the benefit of the establishment?" Answering that "he must do it at the expense of his own private judgment and conscience," Tennent drew the parallel between his case against an established church and that of the colonials against the King, pointing out that "no Legislature under heaven has a right to interfere with the judgment and conscience of men in religious mat-

The graveyard at Circular Congregational Church

ters." He then went on to say, "Dissenters are tolerated, they worship as they please, as do Jews. But is bare toleration equality? Is bare toleration sufficient for the majority of a free state, of a free state that expects to gain its liberties by the sword? Is this equality?" Many members of the Church of England as well as Dissenters signed Tennent's petition, and the new South Carolina Constitution of 1778 placed all Protestant congregations on the same footing. By the constitution of 1790 the people secured a total separation of Church and State.

Circular Congregational Church
150 Meeting Street

May this church long stand, not only as a monument to filial zeal, but as a witness that the truth for which the fathers exiled themselves across unknown seas, to savage wilds, has lost none of its preciousness to their children.
Dedication of the new Circular Church, 1892, as reported in the *Charleston News and Courier*, January 18, 1892.

Circular Congregational Church, as it is now called, was originally the Independent Church of Charles Towne, established in 1681 by some of the first settlers of Charleston. It was the earliest dissenting church in South Carolina and one of the first two congregations established in Charleston, the other being St. Philip's Church. Its first members included Huguenots from France, Presbyterians from Scotland and Ireland, and Congregationalists from England and New England. For over three centuries this church overcame the ravages of wars, fires, hurricanes, and an earthquake. The church was rebuilt three times on the same location. Spiritually, the congregation remained true to its dissenter origins as it dealt with state religion, women's rights, desegregation, and other social issues.

The first building, of white brick, was known variously as the Presbyterian Meeting House and the White Meeting House, from which came the name of Meeting House Street, now Meeting Street. The members called the church Presbyterian, Congregational, and Independent at one and the same time.

The sanctuary at Circular Congregational Church

In 1732 a much larger building was completed. The church became known for its support of religious freedom. One year earlier a group of twelve Scottish families had withdrawn peaceably and built the Scots Kirk, now First (Scots) Presbyterian Church, two blocks down Meeting Street.

In 1772, under the leadership of the Reverend William Tennent, a second church was begun on Archdale Street. Tennent was an arch supporter of the doctrine of the separation of Church and State and was largely responsible for its being written into the State Constitution in 1778. Once this second building was finished, in 1787, an additional pastor was secured, and for thirty years thereafter two sermons were delivered in each of two churches every Sunday. In 1817 the second church separated as the Second Independent Church and later adopted the name Unitarian.

With increasing church membership, the building on Meeting Street was torn down and the first Circular Church was completed in 1806 from the designs of the celebrated architect Robert Mills. This building, in the Pantheon style, accommodated up to two thousand people. It was lit entirely by candles. It was said that it took two and one half hours to light and put out the candles. The Circular Church was described by one observer in 1818 as the "most extraordinary building in the United States." It was originally towerless, and the object of ridicule as a result, until it gained a tower in 1838. It was attended by both whites and blacks and was the site of the first Sunday school in South Carolina, beginning in 1816. Lance Hall was built next door in 1821 and thereafter housed the Sunday school.

In 1861, a great Charleston fire swept across the city and destroyed the church. In 1867 black members asked to be dismissed to form Plymouth Congregational Church, which continues to be a sister church to Circular Church.

The ruins of the burned church stood until the earthquake of 1886. Then, with the old brick and on the same site, the present and fourth building was erected in 1891–92. This is also circular in form but Romanesque in style.

Inspired by the work of Henry Richardson and designed by Stephenson and Greene of New York City, the building combines two powerful forms: the circle (exterior plan), reminiscent of the former church and universal symbol of eternity and wholeness, and the Greek Cross (interior plan), Christian symbol of death and resurrection.

The church's graveyard is the city's oldest burial ground, with monuments dating from 1696. Some of the stones near the church were cracked by the intense heat when the church burned in 1861. Some gravestones are signed examples of noted New England stone carvers, including the only signed example of William Savory, a noted stone carver from Boston. The graveyard holds the grave of Nathaniel Russell, who built the magnificent house at 51 Meeting Street.

The twentieth century at Circular Congregational has been a time of continued independent thinking and social action but also of declining membership. Early in the century this church led others in seeking the right for women to have full voting membership, which was granted in 1908. A turbulent period in the early 1960s saw a schism in the church when some members left upon its adoption of an open-door policy of allowing blacks to worship there. Later in the '60s and into the '70s, the church offered refuge to runaways, initiating a telephone hotline intervention service, and opened a marriage and family counseling center.

In 1961 Circular Congregational joined the United Church of Christ. It simultaneously maintained its affiliation with the Presbyterian Church in the U.S. and the United Presbyterian Church of the U.S.A. Dr. David Ramsay wrote in his 1815 history of the church, "It was never so much its intention to build up any one denomination of Christians as to build up Christianity itself."

French Huguenot Church
136 Church Street

Que ton regne vienne;
Que ta volonté soit faite, sur la terre comme au ciel.
The Lord's Prayer, excerpt from Huguenot Liturgy

French Huguenots were, like the Presbyterians, followers of John Calvin, the sixteenth-century French religious reformer. The Reformation in France was characterized by religious wars between Catholics and Protestants until the Huguenot king Henry of Navarre was able to begin the peace process by initiating religious freedom. The Edict of Nantes, drawn up in 1598 by Henry's committee of scholars and diplomats, extended religious rights to both Catholics and Protestants. After Louis XIV revoked the Edict of Nantes in 1685, France saw a massive flight of Protestants to other countries, including America. The Carolinas, Virginia, Pennsylvania, New York, and Massachusetts were settled by Huguenots.

On April 30, 1680, the English ship *Richmond* brought forty-five Huguenots to Oyster Point with orders from King Charles II that the settlement be renamed Charles Towne. The voyage of these French refugees was subsidized by King Charles for the establishment on British territory of craftspeople "skilled in ye manufacture of silkes, oyles, wines, &c," industries that had been French monopolies. The silkworms did not survive the voyage, but the new arrivals included expert farmers, grape growers, wine makers, weavers, brick makers, and other tradespeople.

The Huguenots also brought their own pastor with them. The Huguenot Church of

Charleston was organized in 1681, and the Reverend Phillip Trouillard is believed to have conducted the first Huguenot service in Charleston. In 1687 the Reverend Elias Prioleau became the first regular pastor of the "French Church of Charles Towne."

The first Huguenot church structure was built on the southeast corner of Church Street and Queen (then called Dock Street). Since water flowed up to East Bay Street and Dock Street, worshipers could come down the Cooper River as the morning tide went out and moor their boats very near the church. When the Council of Province ruled that all Charles Towne churches must begin morning services at 9:00 A.M. and afternoon services at 2:00 P.M., the Huguenots appealed to the Lords Proprietors, stating that "for the convenience of such they began their Divine worship earlier or later as the tide serves."

Groups of Huguenots continued to arrive in the area between 1680 and 1763, settling as far as a hundred miles north and west of the city. When the Church Act of 1706 established the Anglican Church as the principal religion in South Carolina, ten parishes were created under the Bishop of London, coexisting with French Huguenot congregations already formed. Thus the large numbers of French Protestant settlers and their intermarriage with the English in Carolina had a major influence on the Episcopal Church and the development of the colony. Although the old Huguenot parishes were eventually absorbed into the Episcopal Church, the Huguenot Church in Charleston is an exception; it is the only remaining independent Huguenot congregation in America.

The original church building was blown up in an unsuccessful attempt to stop a fire from spreading through the city in 1796. The next, a simple brick structure, was completed in 1800 and then torn down in 1844 to make way for the present building. Built in 1845, it was Charleston's first church in the Gothic Revival style. It was designed by Edward Brickell White, a Charleston architect known for pio-

The French Huguenot Church

neering the rebirth of the Gothic style in America. The contractor, Ephraim Curtis, was one of a line of Charleston master builders.

The church structure, a decided departure from Charleston's earlier architecture, is of stuccoed brick with slender buttresses surmounted by elaborate pinnacles between each bay. The groined ceiling with its rosettes, and the narthex, separated from the nave by a pierced wooden screen of lancet arches, are characteristic of White's design style. A narrow flight of stairs leads from the narthex to the gallery above it, now used by the choir. Marble tablets memorializing prominent Huguenot families line the walls.

The church was damaged by shelling during the Civil War. Later it was almost demolished by the 1886 earthquake but was restored with funds donated by Charles Lanier, a New York Huguenot.

The famous Tracker organ, restored in 1967 by the Preservation Society of Charleston and the Charleston Chapter of the American Organists Guild, is one of Charleston's musical treasures. Made by Henry Erben, a New York organ maker, the instrument is one of the last of its kind in America.

The Huguenot Church uses a liturgy adapted from the French Protestant Churches of Neuchâtel and Vallangin. Services have been conducted in English since 1835, but a service is held once a year, usually on the last Sunday in March, using the archaic French liturgy.

Quaker Meeting House
King Street, south of Queen

True godliness does not turn men out of the world, but enables them to live better in it, and excites their endeavours to mend it.
William Penn, 1682

Important among the religious dissenters in the first hundred fifty years of Charles Towne were the Quakers. Today the only physical reminder of their earlier presence is a section of a wrought iron fence on King Street, just south of Queen, which once surrounded the "Quaker lot" and its successive meeting houses and cemetery. As is indicated on Edward Crisp's 1704 map of Charleston, the Quakers erected one of the first five religious buildings of Charleston.

Originating in England and inspired by their first leader, George Fox, Quakers made their way into the colonies as early as the 1670s. To the north, the Quaker William Penn established Pennsylvania. Farther north, in New England, the Quakers suffered considerable religious persecution. It was this persecution that gave rise to their movement into the colony of Carolina and into Charleston.

Quakers were prominent in early Charleston, among them the famed Mother Mary Fisher Bailey Crosse. A young maidservant in London, Mary Fisher set out on a journey to Turkey, hoping to convert its sultan to Christianity. Failing in that, she traveled to Massachusetts by way of Barbados. In Massachusetts she was jailed, her books were confiscated and burned, and she was deported back to Barbados. After she married a British sea captain, she eventually settled in Charleston, where she was widely known and respected as Mother Mary Fisher. She died there in 1698 and was buried Quaker-style, in an unmarked grave, in the Quaker graveyard on King Street.

Another of the earliest Quakers was John Archdale, who served as the Governor of Carolina from 1694 to 1696. Concurrently Quakers dominated the General Assembly. A section of Charleston where Mary Fisher Crosse and her husband owned extensive property, Archdale Square, gave rise to the present Archdale Street. It

is presumed that Governor Archdale attended the first Quaker meeting in Charleston.

No one knows exactly when the original meeting house was built, though it is believed to have been around 1682. The Quakers may have met under a tent of sail cloth until they erected this building. Some believe they may have met briefly in the Independent Church, or White Meeting House, now Circular Congregational.

The Quaker Meeting House on King Street was active for about one hundred fifty years. The building was roughly 21 feet square. It had a piazza supported by three columns on the south side. Dozens of Quakers were buried at the graveyard on that site. The wooden structure later went through periods of neglect and almost total disuse. In 1838 it was blown up with gunpowder to prevent the spread of a fire that broke out nearby.

A brick building was erected on the vacant lot in 1856 by Quakers from Philadelphia, since apparently there were no Quakers living in Charleston. The building was constructed to prevent the land from escheating to the state of South Carolina. The new building was destroyed by fire in 1861.

The gradual decline of the use of the Meeting House and of the Quaker presence in Charleston seems to have paralleled the Quakers' continuing moral opposition to slavery and their migration to friendlier surroundings. The Charleston Friends Meeting was reestablished in 1982, following an absence of almost a century and a half.

TWO

Episcopal Churches
Founded Before 1800

The English settlement that arrived at Albermarle Point in 1670 soon began to make plans for a permanent city, with walls for protection from the Spanish. Years before, the Spanish had built a walled city at St. Augustine, Florida, to protect themselves from the English. After the settlement transferred to Oyster Point, the first Anglican Church, St. Philip's, was built in 1680 within the city walls on the present site of St. Michael's Episcopal Church. By 1690 Charles Towne, a thriving seaport and trading center, was the fifth largest city in America.

The Royal Charters of King Charles II of England establishing the holdings of the Lords Proprietors in the Carolinas included provisions for the regulation of public religion, assumed to be the authority of the Church of England. However, the Earl of Shaftesbury and John Locke included a set of Fundamental Constitutions for the colonists, giving conscientious dissenters the greatest religious and civil freedom that was to be found in Colonial America.

Ten original parishes were created in the Carolina Colony under the Bishop of London when the Church Act of 1706 established the Church of England as the official religion. These were St. James Santee; St. Philip's; Christ Church; St. Thomas; St. Denis; St. John's, Berkeley; St. James Goose Creek; St. Andrew's; St. Paul's; and St. Bartholomew's. Two of the ten parishes, of French Huguenot origin, were

A *visiting priest enters St. Philip's for a weekday service.*

among congregations already in existence in 1706. St. George's, Dorchester, came out of St. Andrew's Parish in 1717; St. John's, Colleton, from St. Paul's in 1734; St. Michael's from St. Philip's in 1751; and St. Stephen's (English Santee) from St. James Santee in 1754.

The transformation of the Church of England in South Carolina from loyalist Anglican to Protestant Episcopal did not occur all at once with the Revolution. The issue of episcopacy was a difficult one, and many parishioners would have preferred to keep the rank

and privilege afforded to the established church, supported in part by church taxes. Many of Charleston's leading political figures were both patriots and members of the Church of England. Christopher Gadsden, Charles Pinckney, and William Henry Drayton, all Anglicans, were in the emerging nation's political vanguard, believing that the separation of Church and State was paramount to the new government.

St. Philip's Episcopal Church
146 Church Street

For over three hundred years St. Philip's, the mother church of the Episcopal Diocese of South Carolina, has been a vital and cohesive force in the religious, cultural, and civic life of Charleston. Despite the ravages of war, enemy occupations, devastating fires, earthquake, hurricanes, and pestilence, St. Philip's has not only survived but continued to grow to its present membership of over 1,500 communicants. Thus it is today a living link between a courageous past, a lively present, and a promising future.

The name chosen for the parish by the founders was probably taken from the name of the Anglican parish in Barbados, where many had lived on their immigration from England. The first official use of the name St. Philip's appears in the deed recorded in 1697, when the parish acquired an eastward extension of its churchyard. The first St. Philip's Church was built in 1680–81 on the site of the present St. Michael's Episcopal Church at Meeting and Broad Streets. It was located just inside the main entrance to the original walled city and appears on early maps as the English Church. Built of black cypress on a brick foundation, the church was large and stately, surrounded by a white palisade.

After Charleston was established, it was realized that the true entrance to the city was Dock Street (present-day Queen Street), since most new arrivals came by sea . Thus in 1710

the General Assembly authorized construction of a brick church building in a new location to replace the original wooden church. This second edifice, modeled after a Jesuit Church in Antwerp, was built on the site where the third structure was later built and the present church now stands. The first service was held in this second building on Easter Sunday 1723. The exterior architecture of the second edifice was similar to the present structure with the exception of the steeple, an 80-foot-tall tower surmounted by a dome. Services continued in the second St. Philip's until it was destroyed by fire in February 1835. Two paintings of this building by John Blake White hang in the narthex of the present church, the cornerstone of which was laid in November 1835. Services resumed in May 1838. The new nave was built upon the foundation of the former one.

In designing the interior of St. Philip's, Joseph Hyde was influenced by the neoclassical arches inside St. Martin's-in-the-Fields in London, designed by James Gibbs in 1721. Edward Brickell White designed the steeple in 1847 to accommodate a gift of an eleven-bell chime and a musical clock. The original bells, the largest of which weighed five thousand pounds, were later given to the Confederacy for artillery purposes. During the siege of 1864, the 200-foot spire was used as a sighting range for Federal artillery. The church was struck ten times, damaging the interior. Between 1893 and 1915 the steeple was lighted at the top as an aid to ships entering the harbor.

Following a fire in 1920, Albert Simons was commissioned to enlarge the present chancel and sanctuary to accommodate an organ chamber and choir stalls. In the process, he increased the height of the dome over the sanctuary to match that of the vault of the nave.

One may trace the evolution of Charleston's history by reading the names in the churchyard and on memorial plaques around the walls of St. Philip's. Prominent among them are early provincial governors of the Province of South Carolina; Colonel William

St. Philip's Episcopal Church at Christmas

Rhett, Officer of the Crown; Edward Rutledge, signer of the Declaration of Independence; Charles Pinckney, signer of the U.S. Constitution; the Right Reverend Robert Smith, first bishop of South Carolina and sixth American bishop; the Right Reverend Christopher Edwards Gadsden, first bishop to be born in Charleston; three other Episcopal bishops; the Hon. John C. Calhoun, United States statesman and vice president; DuBose Heyward, author of *Porgy*; Henrietta Johnson, noted for her pastel portraiture; and Edward McCrady, distinguished historian. The father of Methodism, John Wesley, preached at the second St. Philip's in 1737, and George Washington attended services there on his visit in 1791.

Pompion Hill Chapel reflected in the East Branch of the Cooper River

Pompion Hill Chapel
On the eastern branch of the Cooper River,
west of Huger

Built c. 1763 as a chapel of ease to St. Thomas Parish, Pompion Hill replaced an earlier wooden church built in 1703. The present structure is a Georgian-style one-story church, rectangular in plan with a slate roof. The walls are laid in Flemish bond. Center doors are located on both long sides. Doors and windows have fanlights topped by brick arches. A small rectangular chancel with a large Palladian window, flanked by smaller arched windows, projects from the east wall. This is balanced by a similar treatment of the vestry room on the west wall.

The bricks for the church came from Zachariah Villeponteaux, brick maker and builder from Parnassus Plantation, who etched his initials into four of the door-face bricks. William Axson was the brick mason, and his initials and Masonic devices are also etched into the bricks. Red floor tiles were donated by the Manigault family of Charleston. Carved native red cedar was used for both the pulpit, situated at the west end opposite the altar and communion table, and the interior woodwork. The

pulpit, carved by William Axson, has an affinity with the pulpit of St. Michael's Church in Charleston, of which Axson was a member.

As the chapel of ease, Pompion Hill served residents of the northern section of St. Thomas and St. Denis Parish who could not easily travel to the parish church. As services became less frequent, Pompion Hill declined in use, experiencing periods of neglect. It has not gone long, however, without regular preservation efforts. It was restored in the early 1960s and remained in good structural condition until erosion problems from the Cooper River began in the 1970s. There has been a continuing effort to stabilize the foundations and control the erosion since that time. The church was designated a National Historic Landmark in 1970. It was carefully restored following the 1989 hurricane.

Interior view of Pompion Hill showing the pulpit and unusual arrangement of the pews

St. Thomas and St. Denis Episcopal Church
Near Cainhoy

St. Thomas and St. Denis parishes were originally distinct from one another. The French Church of St. Denis, named after the patron saint of Paris, was one of the earliest Huguenot congregations established in America after the revocation of the Edict of Nantes in 1685. The French settlement, called Orange Quarter, extended from French Quarter Creek to the Cooper River. This geographic area fell within the boundaries of St. Thomas Parish, established as one of the ten original Anglican parishes by the Church Act of 1706.

St. Thomas Parish Church was built near Cainhoy c. 1706, at which time the two parishes were combined by an enactment of the English Assembly. The act stated that "the French Congregation of the Church of St. Denis, only shall be liable to the Charges and parochial Duties belonging to the said Church, during the time that the Divine Service of the said Congregation be in the French Language, and that for the future, when the Service shall be performed in the English Language, the said Church of St. Denis shall become a Chapel of Ease to the said parish Church of St. Thomas." In 1747 Pompion Hill Chapel replaced the Church of St. Denis as the chapel of ease. The two congregations continued to remain distinct until the death of the Reverend Jean Jacques Tissot in 1768. By that time most of the French congregation had learned to speak English and had been assimilated into the Anglican congregation of St. Thomas and St. Denis.

St. Thomas and St. Denis Parish Church was destroyed by fire from a "conflagration in the woods" in 1815 and was rebuilt in 1819. The small vestry building to the rear of the church is the older of the two structures presently on the site, dating to the original construction. In 1876 St. Thomas and St. Denis was the scene of the Cainhoy Massacre, a bloody racial conflict. Tradition has it that the sanctuary was used as a hospital while the yard and rectory served as an armed camp.

The sanctuary was restored in 1937 by the Colonial Dames with the aid of Harry F. Guggenheim, owner of much of the surrounding land. Dormant since 1925 except for intermittent services, the church has since 1957 been a

T*he balcony of St. Thomas and St. Denis,*
added about 1858

T*he interior of Mount Pleasant's Christ*
Episcopal Church with its wooden ceiling

mission of the Church of the Holy Cross of Sullivan's Island. Since Hurricane Hugo, it has undergone continuing restoration. A number of gravestones dating back as far as 1782 have been restored through a grant from the South Carolina Department of Archives and History.

Christ Episcopal Church, Mount Pleasant
2304 Highway 17 North

Christ Church Parish, Mount Pleasant, was one of ten ecclesiastical subdivisions created in 1706 by the Church Act of the Assembly. Comprising over fifty thousand acres between the Wando River, Awendaw Creek, and the sea, the parish was first served by Christ Church, a frame building whose foundation was laid in 1707. The first services there were conducted in an uncompleted sanctuary the following year by the Reverend Edward Marston, formerly of St. Philip's.

By 1724 the parish had a population of four hundred seventy free persons, "among whom were but a few Dissenters," and more than seven hundred slaves. However, only a fraction of the population were communicants of the church. Since Christ Church was the only public structure in Mount Pleasant, it served various municipal functions until it burned in 1725. Work began almost immediately on a new brick structure to replace the original church, and the congregation worshiped in the new sanctuary for the first time in April 1726.

In 1782, during the Revolutionary War, British troops burned the church and the adjacent vestry house, leaving only the masonry walls standing. Although the building was restored in 1787, Christ Church had no rector and was used for worship only irregularly until 1821. In that year a regular congregation consisting of twelve whites and forty blacks was established and a rector hired.

During the Civil War, Confederate troops used the church as a hospital. After the war Federal soldiers stabled their horses in the church and burned many of the interior appointments as firewood. Christ Church was restored in 1874 and again in 1924. The structure that stands today—with the exception of the cinder-block wings, which were added in 1961—would be familiar to an eighteenth-century communicant.

St. James Santee Parish Church
Near McClellanville

Although this beautiful old brick church now stands alone on the old King's Highway among the oaks and pines of the forest, it was once the center of a busy and prosperous community. Located north and south along the Santee River were rich plantations from which rice was shipped in large casks to Charleston to be sent on to England, Holland, Portugal, and France. Carolina rice became famous all over the world as the finest.

The genius of the French and English was never better displayed than in opening up the hinterlands that lay on the three sides of

Christ Episcopal Church, Mount Pleasant

The interior of St. James
Santee, showing boxed pews,
pulpit, and lectern for the
reading of the service

Charleston and building these plantation homes and their churches. Of the plantations that are contiguous to the area, most are associated with famous persons. Hopsewee was the birthplace of Thomas Lynch, Jr., the youngest of the signers of the Declaration of Independence. Fairfield was the home of Thomas and Charles Cotesworth Pinckney. The Wedge was built by William Lucas, son of Jonathan Lucas, the English genius who constructed the first tidal rice mill. Hampton was the home of the Horrys, ancestors of Archibald Rutledge.

The prosperity of the planter is reflected in the beauty and proportions of St. James Santee. The present building, erected in 1768, is the fourth structure built to serve the St. James parish. It exemplifies the early Georgian ecclesiastical style as found in South Carolina. The body of the church is built of brick imported from England, but the columns of the portico are made locally of brick cast into a curve. The high box pews are made of hand-pegged cypress.

The flagstone floor has withstood the ravages of two wars. The vaulted ceiling retains the original plaster work. The original seating plan of the church was revised early in its history. In this change the chancel was moved from its original position under the Palladian window to its present location in the center of the rear wall.

In 1890 a chapel of ease was built in McClellanville to be used during the summer months. This chapel was used year-round beginning in 1912. In 1914 the Colonial Dames placed an iron fence around a part of the old cemetery at St. James, and in 1932 they placed a slate roof on the church.

Since most of the congregation now lives in or near McClellanville, the chapel of ease is still in use. The old parish church, however, is lovingly cared for. An annual communion service is held there in April, drawing together present members and descendants of members long gone.

Old St. James Santee Church has been placed on the National Register of Historic Buildings.

Old St. Andrew's Episcopal Church
2604 Ashley River Road

One of ten parishes established by an Act of Assembly on November 30, 1706, St. Andrew's Parish was, by coincidence, founded on St. Andrew's Day. Construction of the church began in 1706, as evidenced by an inscription over the door that reads "Supervi 1706 J.F:T.R.," possibly referring to Jonathan Fitch and Thomas Rose, early wardens of the church. The church's walls are the oldest examples of Anglican architecture in South Carolina.

The early part of the structure measured 40 feet by 25 feet. By 1723 the congregation had outgrown the space. The church was enlarged in the form of a cross with a slave gallery at the western end. The building was damaged by fire in 1764 and rebuilt the same year.

The parish was one of the wealthiest in the colonies during the growth of the indigo and rice industries. It began to decline, however, after the Civil War, and St. Andrew's was closed upon the death in 1891 of the Reverend John Grimke-Drayton. Except for occasional services, the church remained dormant until 1948. It regained parish status in 1955 and continues into its fourth century as an active congregation of Episcopalians.

While common in English churches, the cruciform floor plan of St. Andrew's is unusual in a colonial church. Several sizes of English and Dutch brick were used. The additions are of local red brick. Timbers and nails were also made on the grounds. A single timber of solid cypress supports the arch. Much of the stone floor and many of the window panes date back to the original church.

The reading desk and the pulpit are Anglican in style. Behind the altar, tablets or reredos of black cypress display the text of the Lord's Prayer, the Ten Commandments, and the Apostles' Creed. These tablets, with the exception of the lettering, are original to the church. They were relettered and mounted about 1820 on the Honduras mahogany capital. The marble basin of the baptismal font is also

The cross-shaped interior of Old St. Andrew's Episcopal Church is fronted with the original eighteenth-century black cypress tablets.

The elevated pulpit at St. James Goose Creek Episcopal Church

believed to be original to St. Andrew's. The base, a later addition, consists of three pelicans, a heraldic device associated with the Society for the Propagation of the Gospel in Foreign Parts, the group that first sent clergy to the parish. A chalice, a paten, and a flagon date to c. 1870.

Old Saint Andrew's Episcopal Church has survived numerous disasters. Few written documents remain. The parochial registers were lost as early as 1820, and long intervals between clergy have contributed to a lack of historical record. The church itself, however, stands as physical evidence of St. Andrew's long history. An extensive architectural study of St. Andrew's was made by the Reverend George Johnson Tompkins, III, in 1990.

Samuel Gaillard Stoney, is stored inside the church for safekeeping.

Among the interesting items found inside the church are the Royal Coat of Arms of Great Britain and the Izard Family hatchment or arms. Many feel the building was spared by British soldiers during the Revolutionary War because the Royal Coat of Arms was displayed in the church. The Izard hatchment, which is seen above the left side door, is one of only two such memorials found today in churches in the United States.

Some of the church's most notable early members were Ralph Izard, Arthur Middleton, and David Deas. These South Carolinians also served as vestrymen and actively supported the church's ministry.

St. James Goose Creek Episcopal Church
Goose Creek

The St. James Goose Creek Church was established as a result of the Church Act of 1706. The coastal area was divided into ten parishes, of which St. James Goose Creek Church was one.

The parish was officially organized on Easter Monday, April 14, 1707. Benjamin Godin donated the land on which the original wooden church was built in 1707. Today's brick structure, enlarged because of the growth in membership, was completed around 1714. The building recently underwent repairs necessitated by weather and vandalism.

The current building is 50 feet long and 40 feet wide. There is one main entrance with two side doors and thirteen windows. The slate roof and rough-cast walls add to the charm of the St. James Goose Creek Church.

Above the main entrance to the church is a copy of a model of a pelican feeding her young. The image was the symbol of the Society for the Propagation of the Gospel in Foreign Parts, an organization that sent missionaries to the Goose Creek area. The first model, a memorial to

St. James Goose Creek

A view of the tile-floored interior
of Strawberry Chapel showing wall
lettering made of pine cone seeds

A window at Strawberry Chapel

St. John's Episcopal Church, Berkeley
(Strawberry Chapel)
Berkeley County
On the western branch of the Cooper River

Strawberry Chapel was originally built to serve the people of lower St. John's Berkeley Parish. Because of the time and hardships involved in traveling, this chapel of ease was erected c. 1725, on land bequeathed by James Child, for the convenience of the parishioners who normally attended the Parish of St. John's, Berkeley, or "Biggin Church" near Biggin Creek. Biggin Church was not restored after a destructive fire, and Strawberry Chapel officially replaced the parish church of St. John's, Berkeley. This situation was quite unusual, as chapels of ease were usually denied parish church privileges.

The chapel is made of brick; its floors are tile. It is rectangular in shape and has an unadorned hipped gable. The anteroom served in early days as the minister's dressing quarters. The facade is composed of a double three-sided door with a fanlight symmetrically placed between the two shuttered, three-paneled windows. Situated upon a higher level is a lovely rosette window.

In 1946 some communion silver which had been buried during Sherman's march through the South was discovered in the area. A silver-gilt chalice, believed to have been brought to America by the Huguenots, is among the priceless treasures belonging to Strawberry Chapel.

One of the most interesting stories of the chapel is that of seven-year-old Catherine Chicken, a young child who boarded in a local school. The schoolmaster is said to have tied her to a tombstone for disciplinary reasons. She was found and untied by a faithful servant. As a result of the incident, the schoolmaster was instructed to leave town.

Today Strawberry Chapel stands as a reminder of those early colonial days. The structure built as a chapel of ease became the parish of the people.

St. Michael's Episcopal Church
80 Meeting Street

St. Michael's Episcopal Church is one of the focal points of ecclesiastical history in Charleston and the South Carolina Lowcountry. If the older congregation of St. Philip's is considered the grandmother of all churches in the region, then St. Michael's must certainly be the wise and venerable grandfather. It is, in any case, the oldest church building in Charleston.

The rapid growth of the population of Charleston in the late seventeenth and early eighteenth centuries resulted in overcrowding at St. Philip's. According to a contemporary source, "As the inhabitants of Charlestown are so greatly increased . . . it was thought necessary at general desire of the whole parish to bring in a bill for dividing the Parish of St. Philip, and erecting a new church and Parsonage House." Thus, on June 14, 1751, the Acts of Assembly directed the forming of the parish of St. Michael.

The cornerstone of the new structure was laid in February 1752, and the church opened for services nine years later, in February 1761. There is some doubt as to the identity of the architect who designed St. Michael's. Early documents refer to a "Mr. Gibson"; however, information on him is sketchy. He may have been John Gibson, an architect who practiced in South Carolina and died in 1799. The documents may also have referred to James Gibbs, an English architect who published *A Book of Architecture* in London in 1728. Gibbs is best known as the designer of St. Martin's-in-the-Fields in London, which St. Michael's resembles in some respects.

If there is mystery surrounding the identity of the architect who provided the original design of the church, credit for completing the project clearly goes to Samuel Cardy, who, upon his death in January 1774, was eulogized by the *South Carolina Gazette* as "the ingenious architect, who undertook and completed the building of St. Michael's Church in this town."

The church has remained essentially unchanged over the centuries with the exception of the addition of a sacristy in 1883. However, the structure has undergone major repairs on several occasions because of natural and man-made disasters. The steeple tower sank eight inches and the church was cracked in several places by the devastating earthquake that struck Charleston in 1886. St. Michael's was also damaged by a tornado in 1935 and, most recently, by Hurricane Hugo in September 1989. During both the American Revolution and the Civil War, the spire was painted black to make it a less tempting target for enemy gunners. Nearly invisible against the night sky, the building suffered no harm during the Revolution and received only one direct hit from Union artillery batteries in the Civil War. Unfortunately, that shell, which is believed to have been fired from the famous *Swamp Angel* on Morris Island, destroyed the east end of the chancel.

St. Michael's Episcopal Church, the oldest church edifice in Charleston

I nterior view of St. Michael's showing its original
pulpit and massive sounding board and the Tiffany
window depicting St. Michael slaying the dragon

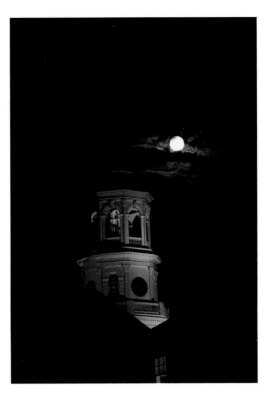

St. Michael's spire at night

The bells of the church, eight in all, were ordered in 1764 from the London firm of Lester and Pack. In December 1782, as the British occupation of Charleston was coming to an end, a Major Traille of the British army removed the bells and shipped them to England, where some years later a Mr. Ryhiner, a merchant who had formerly resided in Charleston, bought them as an investment and shipped them back to South Carolina. However, tradition tells us that once the bells arrived in Charleston, the parishioners of St. Michael's seized them and reinstalled them in the church steeple with no further thought of Mr. Ryhiner. At the outbreak of the Civil War, they were removed once again and sent inland to the state capital at Columbia, where they were thought to be safe. When Columbia was burned in early 1865, the bells were seriously damaged. They were then sent back to England to be recast, after which they were hung once again in the steeple. In 1992 during the restoration work after Hurricane Hugo, the bells made their sixth Atlantic voyage, returning to England for repair. The clock and bells were to be reinstalled in 1993.

The church has been associated with many distinguished people over the years. During his visit to Charleston in 1791, President George Washington worshiped at St. Michael's, where he sat in the governor's pew. In later years the same pew was occupied by other famous guests including the Marquis de Lafayette and Gen. Robert E. Lee. Buried in the churchyard are several distinguished members of the congregation, including Gen. Charles Cotesworth Pinckney, Revolutionary hero, signer of the Constitution, and Federalist presidential candidate; John Rutledge, signer of the Constitution and member of the U.S. Supreme Court; and James Petigru, the famous Charleston Unionist who has been described as the greatest private citizen that South Carolina has ever produced.

Sheldon Chapel Ruins
Near Gardens Corner

There is a 1736 reference to an early chapel "on the South Side of Combahee River, near Hoospa Neck." Sheldon Chapel was commissioned when Prince William's Parish was split from St. Helena, Beaufort, in 1745. A brick temple-form structure completed around 1751, Sheldon was named for the nearby plantation Sheldon Hall, home of Lt. Gov. William Bull. The chapel had thick colonnaded walls of Flemish bond, a portico of molded brick Tuscan columns located on the western end, and a large Palladian window above the altar at the eastern end.

Because the Bull family home was reported to have been a Revolutionary stronghold in 1779, Sheldon was burned by British troops. The chapel was restored in 1824 but was burned again in 1865, this time by Union troops. Sheldon Chapel has since rested in ruins, although the site has continued to serve as a place for memorial observances.

Trinity Episcopal Church, Edisto Island
Highway 174

The picturesque red and white structure of Trinity Episcopal Church was built in 1880, but it represents a history of the Episcopal Church on this rural island that stretches as far back as 1706.

The original parish, St. Paul's, Stono, was one of ten authorized by the Church Act of 1706. The Anglicans of the Edisto vicinity worshiped at St. Paul's. In 1734, Edisto Island was removed from the parish and united with Wadmalaw and Johns Island as St. John's Colleton Parish.

It was not until 1774 that a church building was erected on Edisto, at the site now occupied by Trinity. The congregation was reorganized in 1793 as a separate church that was incorporated by the South Carolina General Assembly as the Episcopal Church on Edisto Island, the name by which it has been known officially since then. In that year, the Reverend James Connor became the first full-time rector. Most of the islanders,

Ruins of Sheldon Chapel of Prince William's Parish, near Gardens Corner

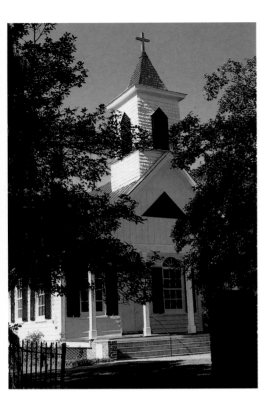

*Trinity Episcopal Church,
Edisto Island*

*The thoroughly wooden
interior of Trinity Episcopal*

however, were not Anglican, there being strong Presbyterian, Baptist, and Methodist groups; in 1812 the parish register showed only fifteen communicants, twelve whites and three blacks.

In 1826 a chapel of ease was built in Edingsville Beach, near what is now Edisto Beach and named St. Stephen's Chapel. Through the years both Presbyterian and Episcopal summer residents shared the chapel, but not without much discord and disagreement. The hurricane of 1893 destroyed Edingsville, its cottages and chapel, and most of the small island itself.

A newer structure, with a gallery for two hundred and a steeple 100 feet tall, was dedicated for Trinity in 1841. A Sunday school was held for blacks. The church at Edisto had striking similarities to St. Michael's, with a gallant portico and a soaring steeple.

The congregation gradually increased, but in 1861, with Union troops advancing from the Beaufort area, the white congregation fled from Edisto. Federal troops used the steeple as an observation post. The congregation reorganized after the war and by 1870 had thirty white and one hundred twelve black communicants. In 1876, sparks from a fire in a nearby field spread and burned Trinity almost completely.

The present structure was erected in 1880. Its fine interior woodwork is of different shades of local heart pine. It was the artisanship of a former slave of the Reverend Seabrook, who educated the artisan in Greek and Latin and trained him as a cabinetmaker. The stained-glass window in the chancel, featuring three women at the tomb of Jesus, stands brilliant in its color next to the golden brown of the polished tongue-and-groove interior work. The hurricane of 1893 did extensive damage to the total structure, but the church was successfully rebuilt. In 1896 and again in 1906 lightning struck the chancel and side entrance.

THREE

Baptist

The South's earliest Baptist congregation was organized in 1682 in Kittery, Maine, under the sponsorship of the First Baptist Church of Boston. Late in 1686, its pastor, William Screven, and twenty-eight of its members moved to the Charleston area and settled on the Cooper River at a place they named Somerton. Baptists from southern England and from Scotland were drawn into William Screven's church when they arrived.

As Charleston grew, many of the church members at Somerton moved into the city. Soon the church was moved there also. Meetings were held in the house of William Chapman on King Street until 1699, when William Elliott donated the lot on Church Street, where the present First Baptist Church stands. A frame building was erected on the lot shortly thereafter. By 1708 the membership numbered ninety-eight.

In 1725 a bequest of Lady Elizabeth Blake enabled the church to build a parsonage on the lot. The meeting house fell victim to a storm in 1731 and was repaired by the congregation. When the British seized Charleston in 1780, they used the Baptist meeting house to store salt beef and forage. In 1785 the congregation placed a baptistry in the yard. This building was replaced by the present First Baptist Church.

A storm of doctrinal differences during the 1740s reduced the congregation to a handful. Disagreement between Calvinist and Arminian elements caused the Calvinist group, followers of Screven, to buy a lot across from the meeting

house. By 1749 First Baptist Church had been without a pastor for two years.

Oliver Hart arrived in 1749 to rescue the struggling congregation. He was a young minister from Philadelphia, the center of Baptist life in America at that time. Hart served for thirty years, forming during his tenure the Charleston Baptist Association, the first in the South. When the American Revolution came, Hart united with other Baptist, Presbyterian, Quaker, and Lutheran dissenters in the colony to oppose the established church in South Carolina. He was forced, however, to flee back to Philadelphia.

The Calvinist congregation did not return

The sanctuary of First Baptist Church at Christmas

to the original church until 1787, the year Richard Furman became pastor. By this time the Arminian Baptists had ceased to exist and the old quarrels had dimmed. From 1787 until 1825, Furman led the church, the Charleston Baptist Association, and South Carolina Baptists in promoting education and missions. He was named the first president of the Triennial Convention, the first national Baptist convention in America, in 1814. By 1821 he had organized the South Carolina Baptist Convention, the first state Baptist convention in America. The Baptist Church, however, was stronger in other parts of South Carolina. Of forty-four South Carolina Baptist Churches, only five were in the Charleston area in 1790.

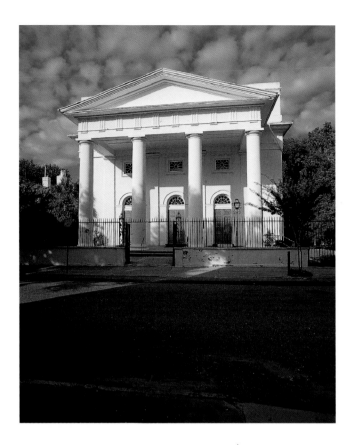

First Baptist Church
61 Church Street

The oldest Baptist Church in the South, First Baptist was begun when its congregation came from Maine in 1686. The present building was erected in 1822, while Richard Furman was pastor. The long-felt need for a new building was realized with a Greek Revival structure designed by the first American-born professional architect, Robert Mills, who said of his design, "The Baptist Church of Charleston exhibits the best specimen of correct taste in architecture in the city. It is purely Greek in style, simply grand in its proportions, and beautiful in its detail." Mills went on to describe the church: "The facade presents a portico of four massy columns of the lightest proportions of the Doric surmounted by a pediment. Behind this portico (on the main walls) rises an attic story squared up to the height of the roof, and crowned by a cupola or belfry. The sides of the building are opened by the requisite apertures for windows and doors, and a full cornice runs round the whole."

With its vaulted ceiling, the interior is grander than Mills' usual style. Materials for a solid mahogany pulpit were brought in from the West Indies for the sum of one thousand dollars.

The history of the building after 1860 has been marked by four events: the Civil War, the hurricane of 1885, the earthquake of 1886, and Hurricane Hugo in 1989. The congregation set to work each time to restore this edifice, and it has recovered from every blow.

In 1883 the pulpit area received extensive modification. In 1966 the church undertook complete restoration and redecoration. As part of this work, the Robert Mills pulpit was reconstructed in the original design, the baptistry was constructed in its present location, and the Wicks pipe organ was installed with all pipes exposed and functioning, a return to the classic concept in organ building.

Citadel Square Baptist Church
328 Meeting Street

Citadel Square Baptist Church is a daughter church to First Baptist Church. It was conceived in the minds of twelve members during evange-

First Baptist, the mother church of Southern Baptists

listic services in spring 1854 when they decided to establish a church in the upper part of the city. These twelve, along with two members of the Wentworth Street Baptist Church (now the site of Centenary Methodist), organized themselves as the Fourth Baptist Church and started worshiping in the chapel of the Charleston Orphan House.

In the following year, the Morris Street Baptist Church, having long struggled with various difficulties, dissolved and united with the Fourth Baptist group. With this union the name Fourth Baptist Church became inappropriate and the enlarged congregation became known as Citadel Square Baptist, which was suggested by the location purchased as a building site.

The present church auditorium was completed in 1856. Because of depressed circumstances following the Civil War, the Wentworth Street church and the Citadel Square church were persuaded to merge in order to advance their cause in the city; they formed the new Citadel Square Baptist Church in 1868.

When a hurricane hit Charleston in 1885, the tower on the church steeple was blown down, the roof was damaged, and the organ was impaired. Before repairs could be undertaken, the earthquake of 1886 struck, causing further damage. The Reverend C. A. Stakely was delegated to go north to solicit funds for repairs. He was successful, although he did not choose to rebuild the steeple to its original height of 220 feet.

Through the years, Citadel Square Baptist Church has become the mother church to many other Baptist congregations throughout the Charleston area, including the Rutledge Avenue Baptist Church (formerly known as the Cannon Street Baptist Church), the Mount Pleasant Baptist Church, the Summerville Baptist Church, the Ashley River Baptist Church, the James Island Baptist Church, and the Folly Beach Baptist Church. Few other churches have such a record of activity in just a hundred years.

The sanctuary of Citadel Square Baptist Church

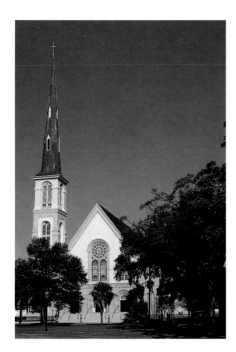

Through the twentieth century a considerable number of improvements have been made at Citadel Square Baptist. These include constructing classrooms, remodeling the auditorium and enlarging its seating capacity to 1,300, moving the organ from the front of the sanctuary to its present location, and installing television broadcasting equipment.

When Hurricane Hugo hit Charleston in 1989, the steeple suffered major damage. This adversity was turned to opportunity when the church decided to return it to its original height and design. Through the efforts of the Friends of Citadel Square Committee, the new 220-foot tower was set into place in 1991, restoring the authentic spire that was once part of Charleston's early skyline.

New Tabernacle Fourth Baptist Church
22 Elizabeth Street

This elegant Gothic Revival structure, home of New Tabernacle Fourth Baptist since 1950, originally housed St. Luke's Episcopal Church, which merged in 1949 with the congregation of St. Paul's Episcopal Church, relocated at the present site on Coming Street, and formed what became in 1962 the Cathedral of St. Luke and St. Paul.

The architect of the church edifice at 22 Elizabeth Street was Charleston's Francis D. Lee, who also designed the reconstruction of the Unitarian Church on Archdale Street. Considered Lee's masterpiece, the Elizabeth Street building was wholly his own creation with no concessions to accommodate an earlier building. Though the exterior structure was left unfinished, with unstuccoed brick and an un-built tower with spire, still it is expressive in its raw state.

The building has a seating capacity of 1,200 and is in the shape of a Greek cross 100 feet by 80 feet. Each side of the edifice presents a single Gothic window 37 feet high. The center of the ceiling, composed of united Tudor arches which spring from the columns, is 55 feet high. There are one hundred two pews on the floor and thirty others in the galleries.

During the Civil War, many shells damaged the church's exterior, and one projectile pierced the roof, passing through the organ gallery and exploding in the cistern. After the evacuation of Charleston, Union troops stripped the church. It was further damaged by the hurricane of 1885 and the earthquake of 1886. Because of the insecurity of the building, services were held by the Reverend Wilson beneath the trees of Wragg Mall. A new organ was finally installed in 1905. In 1908 the sounding board was installed over the pulpit, which came from St. Paul's Church, Stono.

The original New Tabernacle Fourth Baptist Church was founded in 1875 by the Reverend J. A. Chase and was built on the site where the Medical University of South Carolina now stands. This church had been served by the Reverend D. J. Jenkins, who established the Jenkins Orphanage in Charleston. Under his leadership the church was rebuilt in 1904. The Reverend Paul Daniels and his congregation purchased the St. Luke's Church building in 1950 and laid a new cornerstone in 1952 bearing its new name.

Citadel Square Baptist Church, with its spire restored to the original design after Hurricane Hugo

This building is listed on the National Register of Historic Places in Charleston. Its facilities are used frequently by the Spoleto Festival for cultural performances. Such use is most fitting, given the extraordinary beauty and grandeur of this church.

Central Baptist Church
26 Radcliffe Street

Central Baptist Church, constructed in 1891, has been in continuous use since its erection. It is noteworthy in the history of Charleston's churches as the first built and financed exclusively for blacks by blacks. Its structure, which combines elements of octagonal, Italianate, and Gothic architecture, was designed by John Hutchinson and built by members of the congregation. While there are many churches in Charleston built in the 1800s that were used by blacks, most were built on lands given by whites or housed in buildings built by whites. In the case of Central Baptist, the architect was African American, as was the building committee, and all funds for the land and building were raised from the congregation.

The church is also distinguished by its extensive murals, which cover the sanctuary walls and ceiling and depict the story of Christ. These were hand-painted by Amohamed Milai, an obscure artist from Calcutta who was said to be working for the *Washington Post* when members of Central Baptist met him in 1912 at a statewide Baptist convention in Greenville, South Carolina, and engaged him to work on their church. In the murals, which he completed in three years, Milai poured out his testament of an abiding faith. The type of religious art exemplified in this painting is in the medieval tradition of the Italian fresco painter Giotto. It shows a similar style of light-and-shadow and of outlining figures.

Central Baptist is further noteworthy for its central square tower inscribed with the words *Jesus Saves* and topped with an octago-

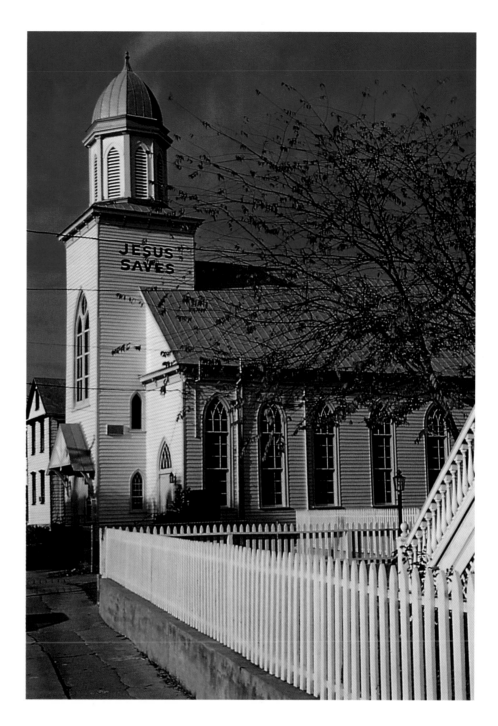

*C*entral Baptist Church on Radcliffe Street

nal spire. The central section of the tower was altered a few decades ago from octagonal to Italianate to keep pigeons from roosting among its louvers, but otherwise the building is unchanged from its original appearance. During Hurricane Hugo in 1989, the steeple was reported to have been lifted into midair by a tornado, spun about, then dropped and smashed on the street below. It was subsequently rebuilt in replication of the original.

*T*he Gothic interior of New Tabernacle was architect Francis D. Lee's masterpiece.

FOUR

Presbyterian

Soon after the founding of Charleston, the community of Presbyterians from Scotland, Wales, and Ireland joined with English Congregationalists and French Huguenots to form the Independent Church of Charleston (c. 1685). Sometimes known as the Presbyterian Meeting House, the White Meeting House was located on the site of the present Circular Congregational Church. The first records of this early church were destroyed by a hurricane in 1713. In his *History of the Presbyterian Church in South Carolina*, Dr. George Howe refers to a letter written from Charleston on June 1, 1710, that describes five Presbyterian churches in South Carolina: "the Church in Charleston being one, and Wilton one, and the other three must be selected out of those of Cainhoy, James Island, John's Island, and Edisto."

In 1731 thirty members, twelve families of the Charleston congregation, withdrew from the White Meeting House to form the Presbytery of Charleston (South Carolina). They built the Scots Kirk, a frame church on Meeting Street south of Tradd in the present location of First Scots Presbyterian Church. In 1811 the Second Church was built to accommodate a growing congregation.

Charleston Presbytery was organized in 1722 and thrived until the Revolutionary War dispersed the ministers and members of its churches. It was reorganized and incorporated in 1790 by the legislature, which was then meeting in Charleston. The Presbytery and its churches became a part of the Presbyterian Church in the Confederate States of America when the nation divided in 1861. In 1865 the

Southern Presbyterian Church merged with the Northern Church, and the denomination changed its name to the Presbyterian Church in the United States. Although the Presbytery and its congregations were never an official part of the Church of Scotland, many of the ministers came to the Presbytery from Scotland and went there for their theological education in preparation for the ministry.

Communion customs followed those of the Church of Scotland. Until 1861 and the advent of the Civil War, communicants desiring to partake of the Lord's Supper left their pews and sat on benches at tables placed in the center aisle of the church, a custom that is continued

T*he interior of Johns Island Presbyterian Church, with its high-boxed wooden pews and hand-carved woodwork* today at the Presbyterian Church on Edisto Island. Preceding Communion Sunday, the members attended a preparatory service held on Saturday afternoon to be presented with "tokens," medallions of silver or bronze. These tokens were collected on Sunday by the elders after the communicants were seated but before they were served, which meant that only communicants who were prepared for Communion could receive it. Black members of the congregation were served in the same manner, following Communion to the white members.

Although white members debated whether racially separating the congregation was to the good, the black membership of Second Presbyterian Church became large enough to form a separate congregation by mid-century. The Presbyterian Church in the United States of America sent Northern missionary representatives into the South because of their concern. A Sunday school was conducted at the Zion Presbyterian Church until Wallingford United Presbyterian Church was erected about 1867. This church was located at 400 Meeting Street between Mary and Reid Streets.

Johns Island Presbyterian Church
Bohicket Road

Johns Island Presbyterian Church was organized in 1710, becoming a member of the first Charles Towne Presbytery established by the Reverend Archibald Stobo in 1722. The earliest pastor of whom there is record was the Reverend Turnbull, who served from 1728 to 1737. In 1793 a house of worship was built on Wadmalaw Island for the purpose of uniting Presbyterians there with those on Johns Island. In 1853 the church had twenty-nine white members and three hundred thirty black members, most of whom were slaves. In 1909 the Wadmalaw church was organized as a separate unit. The church on Johns Island changed its name back to the Johns Island Presbyterian Church in 1925.

The present sanctuary, originally 38 feet long and 35 feet wide, is believed to have been built in 1719. It was enlarged in 1823, and side galleries were added for the black members of the congregation. Bricks for the foundation were imported from England. The risers of the side steps are made of Italian marble. The frame of the church is of heart pine joined by wooden pegs. The siding was handhewn from cypress, and the original roof of black cypress shingles lasted nearly one hundred fifty years.

The original ceiling was of plaster with a 6-foot plaster sunflower in the center. This was replaced with a wooden ceiling after the 1886 earthquake. The flooring of wide boards and the interior woodwork are hand carved. The sanctuary retains high-boxed wooden pews even though the original 9-foot-high pulpit was lowered.

Legible inscriptions on some tombstones in the graveyard date back to 1811; the vaults are probably older. Some earlier burials took place on the plantations.

The building has survived the Revolutionary War, the Civil War, and the earthquake of 1886. Considered by some to be the oldest continuously used Presbyterian church building in South Carolina, Johns Island Presbyterian continues in a remarkable state of

Johns Island Presbyterian Church is framed with hand-sawed heart pine put together with wooden pegs.

preservation. It is on the National Register of Historic Places and is an American Presbyterian and Reformed Historical Site.

Presbyterian Church on Edisto Island
Highway 174

Founded by settlers from Scotland and Wales, Presbyterian Church on Edisto Island is referenced by Dr. George Howe as one of the five colonial churches of British Presbyterians existing in 1710. An even earlier document, a letter dated 1689, refers to a "Presbyterian meeting on Edisto." A number of Baptist families from Lord Cardross's displaced colony at Port Royal also settled on Edisto Island and worshiped in a common building with the Presbyterians until 1722. The church was a member of the old Presbytery of Charles Towne from 1722 to the American Revolution. The Presbyterian Church on Edisto was incorporated in 1784, four years after joining the Presbyterian Church in the United States.

The original building was replaced in 1807 after an earlier fire. This second building was razed when E. M. Curtis was contracted to make improvements, and the present structure was completed in 1836. It has large fluted columns on the portico, an elegant cupola, and an arched ceiling in the sanctuary. Both white and black residents of Edisto worshiped there until Port Royal fell to Union forces in 1861.

On orders of the Confederate government, white residents evacuated Edisto, leaving freed black residents with the Union troops. These residents continued to worship at the church, electing their own session and pastor. Two years after the war's close several white members obtained from the occupying Federal government a writ returning the sanctuary and grounds to the white members. The black members subsequently established Edisto Island Presbyterian Church

Exterior and interior views of Presbyterian Church on Edisto Island

(1866). Both congregations are now members of Charleston-Atlantic Presbytery of the Presbyterian Church and share some activities, the two churches being located half a mile apart.

The manse was built in 1838 with timbers from the church that had burned several years earlier. It is located approximately one mile from the sanctuary and is the third parsonage to stand on that spot. Graves at the Presbyterian Church on Edisto Island date from 1792. Before that time some church members were buried on their plantations.

The list of pastors who served Presbyterian Church on Edisto Island reads like a Who's Who of South Carolina Presbyterians. The Reverend Archibald Stobo preached on the island between 1704 and 1728. In 1741 the Reverend John McLeod, a native of Scotland, was installed as the first official pastor. Dr. Donald McLeod was pastor after the Revolutionary War until 1821; his descendants are still part of the congregation. Dr. William States Lee arrived in 1821 and served the church for fifty-one years as pastor.

The church still follows the traditional Presbyterian service of the Lord's Supper, in which members and visitors walk forward and are seated at wooden tables, where they receive the bread and wine.

First (Scots) Presbyterian Church
53 Meeting Street

The Scots Kirk (or Scots Meeting House) was organized in 1731 by twelve Scottish families who believed in strict subscription to the Westminster Standards and preferred the Presbyterian form of church government. They withdrew peaceably from the Independent Church of Charleston and held the first service of the Scots Meeting House on June 23, 1734, in a simple frame building just southeast of the present structure.

First (Scots) Presbyterian
Church on Meeting Street

The original building stood in the southeast corner of the present graveyard. It was enlarged once before the Revolutionary War and twice during the ministry of Dr. George Buist (1793–1808). The present church sanctuary replaced the first building in 1814. It is the fifth-oldest church building in the city. More than fifty of the gravestones in the churchyard date from earlier than 1800.

Like that of her sister churches in Charleston, the history of First Scots reads like a cycle of creation, destruction, and restoration. The structure has withstood catastrophic events—hurricanes, tornados, earthquake, and fire. The church bell was donated by unanimous vote to the Confederacy in 1862 and never replaced. Consistent restoration and care have preserved the building since its beginnings, a testimony to Scots Presbyterians' determination.

A noteworthy feature of the sanctuary is the red cedar paneling along the walls, now painted white, made from the doors of the old box pews used before the earthquake. The thickness of the walls measures almost 3 feet.

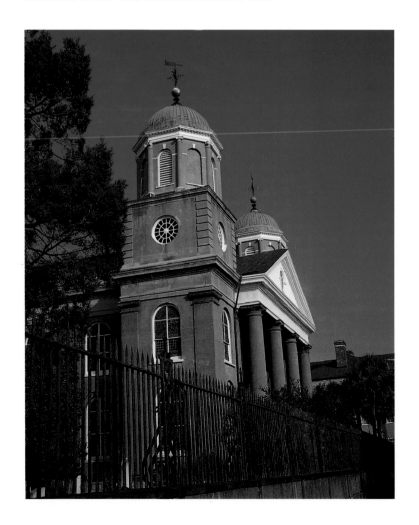

After a fire in 1945, wrought iron grilles with four thistles in the center of each were placed at the front along with a new pulpit and organ.

The carved mahogany baptismal font is believed to date from 1845 and has been copied for Second Presbyterian. A Communion set is dated to 1789, and silver and pewter Communion tokens were used as early as 1800. The stained-glass windows replaced the original clear ones after the earthquake. In the window over the main entrance appears the seal of the Church of Scotland, the Burning Bush, with the Latin motto around the seal: "Nec tamen consumbatur" (Nevertheless it was not consumed).

Second Presbyterian Church

342 Meeting Street

When the congregation of the First (Scots) Presbyterian Church grew to the point that another church was needed, a second congregation was organized in 1809 with the Reverend Andrew Flinn as its first pastor. That same year the group conducted a lottery (a respectable practice at the time) to raise funds for the construction of their church. Two brothers, James and John Gordon, were hired as architects. The Second Presbyterian of the City and Suburbs of Charleston, or Flinn's Church, was completed in 1811 at a cost of $100,000. Wragg Square, the front lawn and park of the church, was dedicated to the people of Charleston as a public park in 1801 by the estate of Joseph Wragg. The Second Church founders bought the site with the understanding that Wragg Square, one of the highest points in the city, would remain an open, public area.

The Second Presbyterian Church building is today the oldest Presbyterian edifice and the fourth-oldest existing church sanctuary in the historic section of Charleston. It is on the National Register of Historic Places. The General Assembly of the Presbyterian Church of the United States met in this building in 1852 when its minister, Dr. Thomas Smythe,

*S*econd Presbyterian Church
at Meeting and Charlotte Streets

offered a resolution that the Presbyterian Church needed to have a historical association to preserve its artifacts and statements of faith. The resolution was passed, forming the Presbyterian Historical Society. Because this happened at Second Presbyterian, the Presbyterian Church of the United States has designated the Charleston church Historical Site Number One of the Presbyterian Historical Society.

In 1854 there were 399 white and 204 black members of the church. The galleries on either side of the sanctuary were used by black members, one of whom left a legacy which is used for missionary work. During the Civil War, two streets bounding the church property

*I*nterior view of First (Scots)
Presbyterian Church

were excavated and the earth was used to fill sand bags for repairs to fortifications on Fort Sumter. Along with those of other Charleston churches, the steeple bell was taken down and given to the state government in Columbia to be cast into cannon.

The building is in the Classical Revival style, built of brick with applied stucco. Features include two tiers of windows, a square tower with an octagonal belfry, pilastered walls, a tetrastyle Tuscan portico, and pediments above engaged columns on the south and north sides. Architect's plans called for a church spire, but the church leaders decided instead on a low dome to defray the increasing cost of the building. The sanctuary was so immense that it was a

strain on the ministers' voices to be heard. In 1833 the floor was raised 3 feet and the ceiling lowered 16 feet. The entrance end of the sanctuary was removed to make an enlarged vestibule on the first floor and a Sunday school above. The north and south entrances were closed to permit the addition of more pews on the sides. Box pews were replaced by the present pews in 1849.

The church survived many of the same natural disasters suffered by First Scots, with the addition of damage caused by the 1813 hurricane. A large stained-glass window behind the altar was destroyed by the 1885 hurricane. Replacement memorial windows were designed around descriptions of the original windows,

The sanctuary of Second Presbyterian Church

lost when the building was unroofed by another hurricane in 1893. In the repairs after Hurricane Hugo the ceiling of the sanctuary was restored to its pre-1833 height.

The silver Communion service, including handwrought tankards and chalice, dates from the time the church was organized. It is still used today along with coin-silver serving trays and implements added over the years. The service was kept in a walnut chest in the home of one of the elders and sent to Columbia for safekeeping when the city was being shelled by Union forces.

Mount Pleasant Presbyterian Church
302 Hibben Street

Mount Pleasant Presbyterian Church, the oldest church organization in its town, was established in 1827 by the congregation of Old Wappetaw Church to serve its members who maintained summer residences along the coast in the village of Mount Pleasant and the surrounding area. The church in Mount Pleasant, fourteen miles south of Old Wappetaw, remained joined to the parent church until it was reorganized after the Civil War. The original church was erected at 226 Bennett Street.

Old Wappetaw had been established as an Independent Congregational Church by fifty-two planters from New England who landed at See Wee Bay in 1696 to claim a land grant. The church evolved into Presbyterianism after a series of Presbyterian ministers. The New Wappetaw Presbyterian Church in McClellanville is its successor.

The building at Church and Hibben Streets that still serves Mount Pleasant Presbyterian was constructed in 1847. During the Civil War, the original pews and pulpit disappeared, and much of the mahogany woodwork was destroyed. The church was used as a hospital by the Confederates and later by the Federals. Notches in the balcony columns were made for holding beds. During the early Reconstruction period, the church building became a school for black children. Later a black minister, the Reverend Thomas Pinckney, was sexton for many years and conducted services for his own congregation on Sunday evenings.

The Charleston Presbytery reorganized Mount Pleasant Presbyterian Church in 1868 and enrolled it in the Synod of South Carolina in 1870. The building was damaged by the 1886 earthquake. Galleries along two sides were closed by an arched ceiling before 1948. Later, doors leading to the galleries were removed and windows installed in their places at each side of the front entrance to the sanctuary. Originally a small balcony just above a window centered behind the pulpit was used for the choir. The choir loft has been relocated several times, and the pews in the sanctuary have been replaced.

The sanctuary underwent a major renovation and enlargement, completed in 1982, that included reopening the balconies, extending the length of the sanctuary, and building a new choir loft behind the pulpit. A Tracker organ,

Mount Pleasant Presbyterian Church

originally built in 1886 and rebuilt by Andover Organ Company, was installed in the choir loft.

Rockville Presbyterian Church
Wadmalaw Island

Rockville Presbyterian Church, erected in 1850, was built on part of the Rockland Plantation owned by Dr. Daniel Jenkins Townsend. Dr. Townsend lived at Fenwick Hall on Johns Island in the winter and summered in the village of Rockville. Although he was a member and elder of the Johns Island and Wadmalaw Church, he found it difficult to attend when he was away in the summer, so he selected a spot in the village of Rockville and built a church with the help of two of his slaves who were apprenticed carpenters in Charleston.

This small white church was built about 11 feet off the ground in the style of the homes of Rockville, with pillars made of tabby, a mixture of shell and lime. It had a slaves' gallery across the back of the sanctuary. Originally there was

The churchyard as seen from Rockville Presbyterian Church.

Rockville Presbyterian Church. The original slave gallery, not visible in this photo, is overhead at the rear.

a tall steeple, but it crashed to the ground in the hurricane of 1893. During the Civil War the steeple was used as a lookout from which to observe Federal gunboats in the North Edisto River.

In 1909 Rockville Presbyterian Church was formally made a separate entity from Johns Island and Wadmalaw Church by the Reverend Paul S. McChesney. Dr. McChesney nonetheless served both churches, as did all subsequent pastors until 1966.

Summerville Presbyterian Church
Laurel Street at Central Avenue

In the late seventeenth century, a group of Congregationalists from Dorchester, Massachusetts, migrated south to form the settlement called Dorchester on the Ashley River. Many of these newcomers spent their summers in another settlement four miles away called Summerville. By 1831 this group built a chapel there for summer services. The winter meeting house in Dorchester continued services until 1866 and was destroyed by the 1886 earthquake.

A meeting of ministers and supporters of the Independent Congregational Church of Dorchester, South Carolina, drew up a petition in 1859 to organize a Presbyterian Church in Summerville. That church consequently became the Summerville Presbyterian Church. Soon thereafter, the Summerville congregation provided sanctuary for coastal residents who fled the Lowcountry when Northern forces invaded. The pastor who served during that period was the Reverend Charles S. Vedder, who later was minister to the Huguenot Church in Charleston.

A new church on the corner of Laurel Street and Central Avenue was erected in 1895 to accommodate a larger congregation. The original meeting house on Central Avenue west of Carolina Avenue is no longer standing.

Summerville Presbyterian's steeple bell was given to the congregation in 1898 by Mrs. E. B. Monroe of Tarrytown, New York, who had attended services at the church when she visited the South. The inscription on the bell reads:

Summerville, S.C.
1898
From the North
To the South
"Peace, good will toward men."

A safe stronghold our God is still,
A trusty shield and weapon.
Martin Luther, 1529

FIVE

Lutheran

Lutheran history in South Carolina is traced to a 1671 colony of oppressed Lutherans from Nova Belgia who were given land on James Island, across the Ashley River from the present city of Charleston. The land is said to have included a plot for a church, although there is no recorded history of this congregation. On May 24, 1734, a Lutheran Communion service was held for the Charles Towne German settlers by the Reverend John Martin Bolzius, pastor of the Salzburger Colony at Ebenezer, Georgia.

By 1742 Melchior Muhlenberg, known as the Father of American Lutheranism, arrived in Charles Towne to work among the German Lutherans. A petition dated August 7, 1753, was made to the Royal Governor for a parcel of land upon which to build a Lutheran church. The petition was denied, but land was eventually acquired. The first Lutheran church was dedicated on St. John the Baptist Day, June 24, 1764, under the name of St. John's.

The German Friendly Society was founded in 1766 by members of St. John's congregation to assist new immigrants and aid widows and orphans. The society continues to the present day.

The German Fusiliers, formed by members of the Lutheran community, were active participants in the Revolutionary War, fighting bravely in defense of Savannah and Charleston. The Reverend Christian Streit, America's first military chaplain, was arrested in 1780 by the British because of his unwavering devotion to the patriot cause. It was he who first introduced English into the worship service.

St. John's Lutheran
Church as restored after
the hurricane of 1989

The golden era of St. John's was the pastorate of the Reverend Dr. John Bachman, whose ministry lasted from 1815 to 1874. Bachman was also an internationally known ornithologist. He extended his ministry to include the black population of Charleston and tutored three black citizens to be Lutheran pastors: Jehu Jones, Jr., who organized an independent black Lutheran congregation in New York in 1836; Daniel Alexander Payne, a bishop in the A.M.E. Church and later the president of Wilberforce University in Ohio; and Boston Jenkins Drayton, the first Lutheran missionary to Liberia (1845), who became chief justice of

St. John's Lutheran Church
on Archdale Street, one of the
oldest original church structures
in Charleston

the Supreme Court of Liberia and governor of the African state of Maryland.

Dr. Bachman made the opening prayer at the convention that drew up the Ordinance of Secession.

St. John's Lutheran Church
10 Archdale Street

St. John's Lutheran Church is Charleston's mother church of Lutheranism. With a history spanning more than 250 years, it is among the oldest congregations of the Evangelical Lutheran Church in America. Organized in 1742, the Lutheran congregation of St. John's worshiped in various places, including the French Huguenot Church, until a wooden structure was built on the present site of St. John's during the period 1759–64. The present church sanctuary on Archdale Street was dedicated in 1817. Frederick Wesner was its architect, and John and Henry Horlbeck were the builders. The steeple, believed to have been designed earlier by Charles Fraser, was erected in 1859.

The church sustained cannon fire during the Civil War, and the parish building was destroyed. Church records and the Communion silver were sent to Columbia for safekeeping but were lost when that city was burned in 1865. The earthquake of 1886 and the hurricanes of 1893 and 1989 also caused damage to St. John's.

The recessed chancel and window were designed by the Reverend E. T. Horn and added in 1896. Mahogany box pews were installed in 1962. The ornamental pipes and case were positioned in the balcony in 1823 by Henry Erben. The present organ was set into the original case in 1965. The original bell, given to the Confederate cause, was not replaced until 1992, when new bells from Paccard-Fonderie de Cloches were dedicated on Easter Sunday.

St. Andrew's Lutheran Church
43 Wentworth Street

St. Andrew's Lutheran Church came into being through a merger of Zion's Evangelical Lutheran Church and the Wentworth Street Methodist Protestant Church. While St. Andrew's dates its history from February 10, 1853, when Zion's Evangelical Lutheran Church was officially organized, the Methodist Protestant congregation was established in 1834, at the present location at 43 Wentworth, when an Independent church split off from the Methodist Episcopal Churches in Charleston.

The portico and wrought-iron gates of St. John's Lutheran Church

St. Andrew's Lutheran Church
on Wentworth Street

The interior of St. Andrew's
Lutheran Church

Zion's Evangelical Lutheran Church became the second English Lutheran congregation when the church was built on Morris Street. The sale of the Morris Street property furnished funds for the repair and renovation of the Wentworth Street building when the two congregations combined after the Civil War. In 1936 the name St. Andrew's Lutheran Church was officially adopted.

The Greek Revival structure that is St. Andrew's Lutheran Church is of stuccoed brick. It has a pedimented portico supported by four Doric columns with decorative ironwork between them. Pilasters between the bays are also in the Doric style, and the sanctuary is in the Greek Revival mode.

In 1908 the chancel was remodeled to have three platforms representing the Trinity. Other features included a lectern, litany desk, altar and raised mahogany pulpit in the shape of a chalice. A sacristy was added on the east side, and the apse was extended to make room for a painting of the Ascension, copied after Peter Biermann by E. Larsen. The stained-glass windows were added during the 1908 remodeling, as well as elaborate plasterwork on the surround of the apse and frescoes on the interior walls. The frescoes were painted over and the plasterwork replaced in a 1936 remodeling. The galleries are original to the building, as is the nave.

The pipe organ, built by Hook and Hastings about 1884, was completely rebuilt in 1944, preserving the original case and many of the pipes. The baptismal font, of German crystal and African mahogany, is of 1839 vintage.

St. Johannes Lutheran Church
48 Hasell Street

In 1841 St. Matthew's Lutheran Church of Charleston contracted with John Sawson, a builder, for the erection of a Greek Revival church on the northwest corner of Hasell and Anson Streets. Edward Brickell White was the architect. The building was completed on June

The doors of St. Johannes at Christmas

15, 1842, and dedicated on June 22. When this congregation moved to what is now St. Matthew's Lutheran Church on King Street, the Hasell Street building was sold to Salem Baptist Church (1872).

In 1878 a group of Lutherans formed a congregation known as the Deutschen Evangelisch-Lutherischen Sanct Johannes Kirche, the German Evangelical Lutheran St. Johannes Church. Its first congregation meeting was held on April 22, 1878, at which time a constitution was adopted and Johannes Heckel of Ohio was called to become the church's first pastor. The initial meetings were held in what was then known as the Hasell Street Chapel near Meeting Street. Soon thereafter, the former sanctuary of St. Matthew's became available. The present church at Hasell and Anson Streets became St. Johannes, holding its first service in October 1878. Services were conducted in German at St. Johannes until 1910.

The exterior of St. Johannes Lutheran is Greek Revival with four massive columns supporting the portico. The church underwent extensive repairs after the 1886 earthquake and

St. Johannes Lutheran Church, Hasell Street, an architectural gem in the heart of Charleston's Ansonborough district

again in 1913, when the interior was remodeled. The 1913 work included the installation of a marble tiled floor and railings around the side galleries, and the enlargement of the choir loft. The circular chancel railing was removed, the chancel floor was redone, and the memorial windows were installed. The 1881 pipe organ was rebuilt in 1920 and replaced in 1949 with a new Austin pipe organ with cathedral chimes. The glass memorial doors at the entrance of the nave were placed in 1958.

Exterior view of St. Johannes Lutheran Church on Hasell Street

St. Matthew's Lutheran Church
405 King Street

St. Matthew's is the second-oldest Lutheran congregation in Charleston, having been organized on December 3, 1840. Shortly after that date, the congregation purchased a lot at the corner of Anson and Hasell Streets and began work on a church building which was dedicated in 1842. With the influx of German immigrants, the handsome Doric structure in time proved too small to accommodate all pew applicants.

In 1868 St. Matthew's bought the lot at 405 King Street just west of Marion Square, and work was soon begun on a new, much larger church. On Holy Thursday, March 28, 1872, a procession of more than 3,000 people marched from the old site on Hasell Street to the new St. Matthew's for dedication ceremonies. As the *Charleston Courier* noted on the following day, "The new German Church—the spire of which points high above all other church spires in the city, is an ornament to the city." The new church, whose 297-foot spire in fact stands taller than any other in the state, was designed by architect John H. Devereux.

After the move to King Street, the members of St. Matthew's sold their original Hasell Street church building to the Salem Baptist Church. It was in turn sold to St. Johannes Lutheran Church in 1878. This congregation continues to meet in the 1842 sanctuary.

*I*nterior view of St. Matthew's Lutheran
Church, showing its stained-glass windows imported from Germany

In the late evening of January 13, 1965, St. Matthew's was severely damaged by a fire. Though the wall structure was left largely intact, the fire destroyed the magnificent spire, which fell into the street. Unsolicited contributions from throughout the United States and Canada helped make possible the complete restoration of the church, including the reconstruction of the spire. The spire was restored again following the 1989 hurricane.

St. Paul's Evangelical Lutheran Church, Mount Pleasant

604 Pitt Street

According to Lutheran records, in 1884 the Church Society of the Concordia Association, which had held meetings in the Mount Pleasant Presbyterian Church since 1881, decided to erect a church on Pitt Street. It was also agreed that the name of the parish would be the German Evangelical Lutheran St. Paul's Parish of Mount Pleasant, South Carolina. Later the name of the church became St. Paul's Evangelical Lutheran Church.

The plans for the edifice were drawn by Professor Frank Muench, whose aim was to reproduce a genuine German village church that would speak to the hearts of his countrymen. James C. LaCoste was the builder. One of the ways the Lutherans raised funds for the work was by holding picnics at Alhambra Park. The German Bank of Charleston furnished music at these gala affairs. While construction was in progress, church meetings were held at the residence of J. H. Patjens.

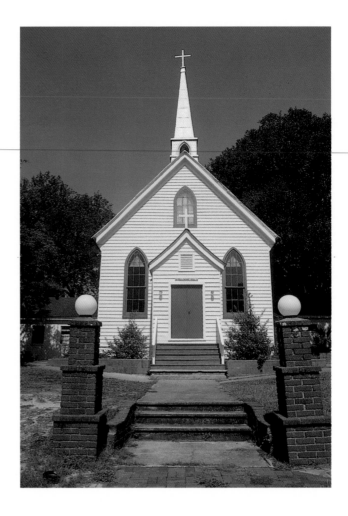

The simple frame structure on Pitt Street has withstood many hurricanes with little damage. St. Paul's congregation eventually outgrew the original sanctuary, and a new church was built next door in 1972. Its sanctuary has a seating capacity of approximately 250, compared to 125 in the old sanctuary. The pulpit and lectern were transferred from the old building to the new; the original pews were sold to members and townspeople when the old church became the fellowship hall.

The original St. Paul's Evangelical Lutheran Church edifice in Mount Pleasant, now a parish hall

*T*his synagogue is our temple, this city our Jerusalem, this happy land our Palestine, and as our fathers defended that temple, that city, and that land, so will their sons defend this temple, this city, and this land.

Rabbi Gustavus Poznanski, at the consecration of the new synagogue on Hasell Street, March 1841

SIX

Jewish

The earliest known reference to Jewish presence in the English settlement of Charles Towne occurred in 1695. Soon thereafter, settlement by other Jews, of Spanish and Portuguese background, followed. This pioneer group knew the indigo trade and was attracted by the ample economic opportunity of the colony, and especially by the promise of civil and religious liberty in Charles Towne. By 1700 there may have been a sufficient number of Jewish residents to form a quorum for worship. The growing influx of Sephardic immigrants from London and Amsterdam enlarged the community in the 1740s. By 1749 the Jewish population was large enough to organize the present congregation,

Kahal Kadosh Beth Elohim (Holy Congregational House of God). Fifteen years later they established the now historic Coming Street Cemetery, the oldest Jewish burial ground in the South.

Until the development of Reform Judaism in Charleston in 1844, the community followed Orthodox doctrine equivalent to that practiced by Spanish and Portuguese congregations in London and Amsterdam. Charleston now has three synagogues; they serve Orthodox, Reform, and Conservative congregations.

Kahal Kadosh Beth Elohim
90 Hasell Street

Kahal Kadosh Beth Elohim (Holy Congregational House of God) is a registered national historic landmark. Regarded as an important example of the Greek revival style in America, it is the oldest synagogue in continuous use in the United States and the oldest surviving Reform synagogue in the world.

Beth Elohim is acknowledged as the birthplace of Reform Judaism in the United States. In 1824 a group of congregants made an unsuccessful attempt to change the Sephardic Orthodox ritual by introducing the English language and abridging the service. The group then resigned from the congregation to organize the Reformed Society of Israelites. The society disbanded nine years later when the progressives rejoined the old congregation, bringing to Beth

*T*he brass menorah of Beth Elohim, given to the congregation in 1802

Elohim a modernist attitude and liberalization of practices.

In 1840 the present Greek revival temple replaced the old 1794 Georgian structure after it was destroyed in the great fire of 1838. An organ was installed when the new synagogue was built, making Beth Elohim the first synagogue in America to include instrumental music in worship.

Beth Elohim has been the religious home of a number of eminent leaders. Moses Lindo developed the fabulous Carolina indigo trade, which brought much wealth to the colony before the Revolution. Joseph Levy was a veteran of the Cherokee War of 1760–61 and probably the first Jewish military officer in America. Francis Salvador became a deputy to the Provincial Congress of South Carolina in 1775 and was the first Jew to hold an important elective office in America. One year later, during the Revolutionary War, he was scalped by

Indians, becoming the first Jew to die in the Revolutionary War.

In 1784 members of the congregation founded Charleston's Hebrew Benevolent Society, the nation's oldest Jewish charitable organization; in 1801 they established the Hebrew Orphan's Society, also the country's oldest. Both are still active. In 1838 Beth Elohim pioneered a new approach to American Jewish education and established the second Jewish Sunday school in the United States, under the direction of Sally Lopez. The blind poet and hymn writer Penina Moise was an early superintendent.

Beth Elohim's present temple was designed by architect Cyrus L. Warner and built in 1840 by member David Lopez, for whom the first submarine, *Little David*, was named. The temple grounds are fronted by a graceful iron fence dating from the 1794 synagogue. The large marble tablet above the huge entrance doors proclaims the Sh'ma in Hebrew. The massive

Interior of Beth Elohim with a view of the open ark and the old silver ornaments of the historic Torah

ark, which by local tradition is kept open throughout worship services, is made of Santo Domingo mahogany. It contains the impressive old silver ornaments of the historic Torah. Also to be found in the interior are brass menorahs (given to the congregation in 1802, lost after the fire of 1838, but found in 1910), an organ, and stained-glass windows replete with Jewish religious symbols.

Next to the temple is Pearlstine Hall, formerly called the Bicentennial Tabernacle, erected in 1950. This auxiliary building replaced the temporary structure that had been hurriedly built after the 1838 fire but had nevertheless remained in use for 111 years. Pearlstine Hall contains a social hall, a gift shop, two large murals by Charleston artist William Halsey, and a pair of wrought iron sculptures of biblical prophets. An archives museum is housed in the adminis-trative building, a reconditioned and expanded eighteenth-century structure to the rear of the temple at 86 Hasell Street.

Brith Sholom Beth Israel
182 Rutledge Avenue

In 1854 a small group of Jews met in Charleston for worship according to the Ashkenazi ritual of Orthodox Judaism. These loyalists consisted of Jewish newcomers from Central and Eastern Europe and a group which had departed Beth Elohim at the height of a controversy centering around the installation of an organ, the first in any Jewish synagogue in America. In 1856 the members of Brith Sholom Beth Israel dedicated their synagogue at St. Philip and Calhoun Streets. Through the years, the congregation grew, and the original synagogue was enlarged and rebuilt several times.

In 1911 differences among the members in Brith Sholom caused a split that resulted in the organization of the Beth Israel Congregation. In 1945 that congregation built a new structure at the juncture of Bee and Rutledge. In 1956 the two congregations merged as Brith Sholom Beth Israel to form what is the oldest Orthodox synagogue in the South and one of the oldest Ashkenazi congregations in America. The year 1956 saw the founding of the Charleston Hebrew Institute Day School, the precursor of the Addlestone Hebrew Academy.

When the synagogue was built on Rutledge Avenue, the beautiful interior of the old St. Philip Street sanctuary was rebuilt into it. The stained-glass windows were moved and reset, the pillars which supported the women's balcony were moved and are still in use. The magnificent Aron Kodesh, the Holy Ark, was moved too and enlarged in its new home. Velvet curtains were hung before it. Three antique chandeliers completed the restoration.

*I*nside Brith Sholom Beth
Israel, the oldest Orthodox
synagogue in the South

*T*he original ark of
Brith Sholom Beth Israel

SEVEN

Roman Catholic

Prior to the American Revolution, there were very few Irish and Spanish Catholics in Charleston, and those few did not make themselves known in the city. In 1786 a vessel bound for South America arrived in Charleston harbor with an Italian priest on board. By this time, thanks to the city's tolerant atmosphere, the Catholic community had increased in number. Twelve of its members invited the Italian priest to celebrate Mass. This he did in the home of an Irish Catholic, possibly located on the northeast corner of Tradd and Orange Streets.

In 1778 South Carolina had declared in the twelfth and thirteenth articles of its constitution that "No person shall be eligible to a seat in the Senate . . . or to sit in the House of Representatives . . . unless he be of the Protestant religion." Charles Pinckney, in his *Draft of A Federal Government* (presented to the 1787 Philadelphia Convention to amend the Articles of Confederation then binding the state together), included the clause "The Legislature of the United States shall pass no law on the subject of religion." The article was amended to read, "Congress shall make no law establishing religion, or to prevent the free exercise thereof." Following Pinckney's initiative, South Carolina capitulated and struck out of its constitution the clauses excluding Catholics and members of certain other religious groups from public office.

The Right Reverend John Carroll, Prefect

St. Mary's, the first Roman Catholic church of the Carolinas and Georgia

Apostolic of the United States, wrote on April 20, 1790, "According to the information sent me from Charleston, the number of Catholics is about 200. Every day they become more numerous. Many—whom past discouragements and oppressions kept concealed—begin to show themselves. Our religion has not been exercised publicly there above two years. The Catholics there are mostly poor. . . . They have no church, but divine service is performed in a ruinous house which they have hired."

The first established site for Catholic worship in the Carolinas and Georgia was St. Mary's, organized in 1789. The arrival in 1793 of 114 French refugees from the French colony of St. Domingo greatly increased the number of

Roman Catholics in Charleston. Among those newly arrived were people of prominence such as Admiral Comte deGrasse and his family. (Two of his five daughters are buried in St. Mary's churchyard.) Additional ships from the West Indies brought in more church members as various insurrections occurred.

The Right Reverend John England, the first bishop of the newly established Roman Catholic diocese, arrived in the city in 1820. It is said that the French contingent of St. Mary's parish was so indignant that an Irishman could be raised to such a position of authority, it initially barred the doors against him. Bishop England, however, soon won Charleston over with his hard work, wit, and eloquence. This did much to mitigate Protestant apprehensions about "Papists."

St. Mary's Catholic Church
89 Hasell Street

St. Mary's Church, the first established Catholic site in the Carolinas and Georgia, was organized in 1789 by the Reverend Thomas Keating by direction of the Right Reverend John Carroll. The first St. Mary's was a wooden building on Hasell Street that had formerly been a Methodist meeting house. It was replaced by a brick building built between 1801 and 1806 which measured about 60 feet by 40 feet and had a small gallery containing an organ. A porch supported by four 25-foot columns was added later.

Between 1810 and 1822 the St. Mary's congregation suffered a troublesome schism be-

St. Mary's interior, showing some of the wall paintings, twenty-three of which are by Roman artist Caesare Porta

tween its vestry and church authority widely known as the "Charleston Schism." By Easter 1819, however, it had 200 communicants, thanks partly to the arrival of many French newcomers from the West Indies. The registers of the church were kept in French until 1822. The present St. Mary's Church opened for worship in 1839, a year after the brick church was destroyed by the fire of 1838. During the Civil War, shelling of the city, in which St. Mary's was struck repeatedly, necessitated the abandonment of the church, and services were held in private residences.

The present edifice of St. Mary's Church was consecrated on March 25, 1901. The consecration ceremony is commemorated each year when the candles under the Stations of the Cross are lighted on the Sunday after the feast of St. Charles.

The church's high altar, Altar of the Sacred Heart, platform, baptismal font, and sanctuary are of polished marble. Twenty-five opalescent mosaic windows were made by the celebrated Royal Bavarian Establishment in Munich. Over the main altar is a Crucifixion painted in 1814 by John C. Cogdell, a native Charleston artist who restored the work in 1839 after the fire. In the sanctuary are twenty-three oil paintings by Roman artist Caesare Porta. The great central painting of the ceiling was placed in 1896.

St. Mary's graveyard, with its international assortment of names, is among the most interesting in the city. Bishop England wrote of "the evidence of the Catholicity of those whose ashes it contains. You may find the American and European side by side. France, Germany, Poland, Ireland, Italy, Spain, England, Portugal, Massachusetts, Brazil, New York and Mexico have furnished those who worshiped at the same altar with the African and Asiatic" and commented that "after death their remains commingle. The family of the Count deGrasse, who commanded the fleets of France, near the Commodore of the United States and his partner, sleep in the hope of being resuscitated by the same trumpet.

The present edifice of the Cathedral of St. John the Baptist, a near-replica of the earlier cathedral structure destroyed by fire in 1861

Cathedral of St. John the Baptist
Broad and Legare Streets

In Cork, Ireland, the Right Reverend John England was consecrated first Bishop of Charleston in September 1820; he assumed his duties in Charleston a year later. The original diocese comprised North Carolina, South Carolina, and Georgia. The first cathedral, a simple wooden chapel known as St. Finbar, was located at Vauxhall Gardens, the area bounded by Broad, Legare, and Queen Streets west of King Street. It is referred to by R. L. Clark as "a rude and weatherboarded church, but which resounded with the richest eloquence in America."

The first Cathedral of St. John the Baptist

and St. Finbar was consecrated on the same property in 1854 during the episcopate of the Right Reverend Ignatius Reynolds. Known as St. Finbar's, it was an outstanding example of Gothic architecture following the trend of the Germans of the fourteenth century. It was built of Connecticut sandstone at great cost and had a 200-foot spire. This grand cathedral was completely destroyed during the 1861 fire. Also destroyed were the adjoining rectory and the library of the old seminary with its 17,000 volumes. Except for the image of St. Finbar looking down from the chancel wall, everything was lost including the church vestments and sacred vessels.

The cornerstone for the present Cathedral of St. John the Baptist was laid in 1890, and the building was finished in 1907. The architect, P. C. Keely of Brooklyn, New York, followed plans that were almost identical to those of the previous cathedral, although the planned spire was replaced by a square tower for monetary reasons. The cathedral is of tool-chisled Connecticut brownstone with a 60-foot vaulted ceiling. A brownstone terrace with Tennessee marble landings and plaza leads up to the main entrance, which has brownstone columns and a high, pointed arch.

Over the main entrance in stained glass is the Coat of Arms of Bishop Northrop. The Papal Coat of Arms and the Coat of Arms of the State of South Carolina appear over the east and west doors. The nave, tiled and measuring 150 feet long by 80 feet wide, seats seven hundred people. White Vermont marble makes up the three altars, the main altar being noteworthy for its carvings. The stained-glass windows were produced by Meyer and Company of Munich. The fourteen large windows along the sides represent the life of Christ, and in the clerestory are windows honoring the four Evangelists. The rose window depicts the baptism of Christ by St. John the Baptist. The five-light panels below the rose are copied from Leonardo's *Last Supper*. Pews, confessionals, and the Bishop's throne are of carved Flemish oak.

The Chapel of the Blessed Virgin, on the

Altar window and chandeliers of St. Patrick's Catholic Church

Cathedral of St. John the Baptist, with its Gothic arches and three white altars of Vermont marble

63

right side of the main sanctuary, contains an altar surmounted by a statue of the Virgin by Pettrick of Rome. There are four one-light windows in the chapel. Two one-light windows on the upper tier represent Mary, the Lily and the Mystical Rose. Built to a similar floor plan, the Chapel of the Blessed Sacrament is on the gospel side of the main sanctuary.

St. Patrick's Catholic Church
136 St. Philip Street

St. Patrick's parish was established by Bishop England on a tract of land purchased in 1828 at the corner of St. Philip and Radcliffe Streets. Ten years later, on St. Patrick's Day 1838, the cornerstone of St. Patrick's Catholic Church was laid. The original frame church was 50 feet in length, 36 feet wide, and 24 feet high, with a sacristy behind the altar. Galleries ran along each side, on the north for blacks and on the south for whites. There was a west gallery for an organ.

The Reverend Patrick O'Neill was the first pastor, remaining at St. Patrick's until his death in 1865.

The cornerstone for the present structure was laid on St. Patrick's Day 1886. (A reenactment of this ceremony took place on March 16, 1986, with the burial of a time capsule.) The building of the church was delayed until 1887 because of the earthquake of August 31, 1886. The architect was P. C. Keely and the builder was H. L. Cade. Twenty windows of cathedral glass light the vestibule, nave, sanctuary, and vestry rooms.

In 1943 St. Patrick's underwent renovations which included the addition of the Chapel of the Blessed Sacrament, donated by Rosa Riley in memory of the Riley family. Box vestries on either side of the high altar were removed and the side altars moved. Additional restoration took place over the years, thanks to the efforts of Father Egbert Figaro. This restoration included increasing the land area of the cemetery and fencing it in with wrought iron.

Ornamental wooden arches of St. Patrick's Catholic Church

Stella Maris, Sullivan's Island
1204 Middle Street

Most Lowcountry historians refer to Sullivan's Island in either a military connection—as the home of Fort Moultrie—or in the context of summers on "The Island," when residents of Charleston made a yearly migration to escape the heat and disease in the city. Unfortunately, these historians overlook the group of mostly Irish settlers who formed the year-round population of the island from its earliest days. Their history is expressed in Stella Maris parish.

Established in 1843 and erected in 1873, Stella Maris was named after Our Lady, Star of the Sea. The present Gothic Revival structure replaced an older frame building, St. John the Baptist Church, built in 1845. John H. Devereux, a Charleston architect and summer parishioner, provided his services for the design of the new building. Brick used in the entrance floor and exterior walls was salvaged from Fort Moultrie following wartime shelling. Obtaining the necessary permission to use this resource, one tradition has it that Father Timothy Birmingham helped chip mortar from the old bricks, often working at it until his fingers bled. The church tower of Stella Maris was added in 1880.

Following a major storm in 1893, restoration produced the present sanctuary interior with panels of cypress and poplar topped with rosettes in the frieze. According to one tradition, the cypress used in the renovations came from a boat that washed ashore during the storm. The ceiling of Stella Maris forms an arched curvature resembling that of a ship's hull. A simplified Baroque dome surmounts a semicircular area for the altar. On either side of the altar, fluted columns support classical capitals with acanthus leaves carved from single blocks of wood. Other classical details were added, including Corinthian columns and a cornice consisting of carved brackets with pendants. During this restoration, a church bell weighing 510 pounds was installed.

Fourteen stained-glass windows depicting Mysteries of the Rosary were placed by Navino Nataloni in 1955 during another period of remodeling. Earlier windows had been damaged by gunfire during training exercises at Fort Moultrie. In the late 1970s the paint and gold leaf were removed from the interior to reveal the heart-of-pine nave and various woods in the sanctuary.

When Hurricane Hugo devastated the coastal islands around Charleston, tidal waters nearly six feet deep rose in Stella Maris, damag-

ing the floors, pews, furnishings, and vestments. Structurally, however, the church fared well, remaining the spiritual home to the descendants of its original families and a beacon to ships as they approach the harbor.

Stella Maris on Sullivan's Island

*A*n interior view of Stella
Maris showing how its ceiling
resembles a ship's hull

EIGHT

Methodist

John Wesley and his brother, Charles, ordained ministers of the Church of England, visited Charleston in 1736. They had been sent as missionaries, with Savannah, Georgia, as their destination. Records indicate that John Wesley preached in St. Philip's Church in 1737. His *Collection of Psalms and Hymns* was printed in Charleston. However, Wesley's stay in Savannah was short. In December 1737 he returned to England, where he laid the foundation for what was to become the Methodist Church.

During the 1740s renowned preachers such as George Whitefield spent time in Charleston, but the official Methodist Church was not started until Bishop Francis Asbury's arrival in 1785. A devoutly religious man who dressed in black, Asbury called Charleston "the Sodom of the South." The Charlestonians' proclivity toward drinking, smoking, card playing, horse racing, dancing, and, worst of all, slaveholding gave rise to Asbury's belief that the Methodist doctrine was needed in Charleston.

On February 27, 1785, Charleston's first Methodist congregation was established. Among the locations where the group met were an old Baptist meeting house on Church Street and Mrs. Stoll's house on Stoll's Alley. In 1786 the Cumberland Street Methodist Episcopal Church, between Meeting and Church Streets, was completed. It was also called the Blue Meeting House. The church's early ministry was the target of much public outcry because of the Methodist belief, originating with John Wesley, that one human should not hold another in

T rinity United Methodist Church on Meeting Street, originally Westminster Presbyterian Church

slavery. The Cumberland Street Church had rocks thrown through its windows, and on one occasion a minister was nearly drowned in a public trough. Despite this animosity, the congregation of Cumberland Methodist Church grew. To make room for its expansion, the first Bethel Methodist Church was built on the corner of Pitt and Boundary (Calhoun) Streets.

In 1791 the Cumberland Church was the site of the fifth session of the South Carolina Methodist Conference. Bishop Thomas Coke arrived in the company of a young Irish minister named William Hammet, who enthralled the

*I*nterior of Trinity United
Methodist Church

Charlestonians with his eloquent preaching. An inspired group of Cumberland's members demanded that Asbury appoint Hammet to their church, but the Bishop had already made the pastoral assignments and refused to change them. Encouraged by Hammet, the group continued to challenge Asbury for several months. Finally, on November 28, 1791, Hammet publicly disavowed "Asbury Methodism" and led half the white members of Cumberland in a walkout. He called his new denomination Primitive Methodism and established Trinity Primitive Methodist Church. Trinity prospered, and Hammet went on to found seven other Primitive Methodist congregations. Only Trinity and St. James (Spring Street) survived beyond Hammet's death in 1803. In 1816, the year of Asbury's death, Trinity and St. James formally joined the South Carolina Conference of the Methodist Episcopal Church in America.

Another theological storm emerged when the congregations of Cumberland and Bethel Methodist Churches suffered increased persecution because of their active education of African Americans. In 1817 this crisis produced a confrontation between the white and black class leaders of Bethel, leading to a changeover of many of the African American membership into Charleston's first A.M.E. congregation. The public perception of the Methodists as abolitionists was furthered by the arrest of Denmark Vesey, one of Bethel's former class leaders, and Charleston's Methodists were held suspect for encouraging insurrection. At this point the church found it necessary to distance itself from pro-abolition politics, although it continued to educate the black members of its congregation.

After the Civil War there was a struggle between the Methodist Episcopal Church, South, and the Northern Methodist Episcopal Church for control of the Charleston churches. For the white members of the congregation, this meant separating from the black members who went with the Northern church. The old sanctuary, Old Bethel, was dedicated to the black congregation in 1876.

Cumberland Street Methodist Church, the mother church of Charleston Methodists, did not survive the destruction of the Civil War; by 1874 it was absorbed officially into Trinity Methodist Church.

Trinity United Methodist Church
273 Meeting Street

When William Hammet publicly disavowed "Asbury Methodism" on November 28, 1791, he led half the white members of Cumberland in a walkout. Later he formed a new denomination that he called Primitive Methodism, gathering his followers in the City Market. On February 14, 1792, he bought a large plot of land for a church building at the southeast corner of Hasell Street and Maiden Lane. There Trinity Primitive Methodist Church prospered. Hammet went on to found seven other Primitive Methodist congregations, but only Trinity and St. James (Spring Street) survived beyond his death in 1803. In 1816, the year of Asbury's death, Trinity and St. James formally joined the South Carolina Conference of the Methodist Episcopal Church in America.

With Hammet's death, Trinity was turned over to William Brazier, who had no interest in keeping the church going. Through a series of arrangements, William Brazier sold Trinity to a dissatisfied minister from St. Philip's Episcopal Church. When the Episcopalians held their service of dedication, an enraged crowd of "Hammetites" tried to reclaim the church, but they were rebuffed by a gun-toting pastor. At a later service a lady from Trinity's Methodist congregation stole the front door key, with which she locked out the new congregation. Hammetites occupied the building around the clock for several months until the courts returned Trinity's ownership to the Primitive Methodists in 1804.

A terrible fire swept across the Charleston

Rosa Parks speaking at the funeral of another civil rights leader, Septima Clark, at Centenary United Methodist Church in 1987

The Tiffany window of
Trinity United Methodist Church

peninsula in 1838, destroying Trinity Church. In December 1838 the cornerstone for the second Trinity was laid. The new Trinity was a larger masonry structure in a compact neoclassical form.

During the Civil War, both Trinity's and Cumberland's sanctuaries were increasingly threatened by the Federal bombardment; the churches had to be abandoned. Trinity's members managed to return after the war, but Cumberland was lost. In 1874 the remnants of Cumberland's congregation were incorporated officially into Trinity. The United States Reconstruction authorities gave Trinity to a black congregation affiliated with the Northern Methodist Church. Trinity's old members sued and regained possession of the building; they invited the black congregation to stay, but only in

the galleries. In response, the Northern Methodists, led by the Reverend T. Willard Lewis, left Trinity and went on to found Centenary Methodist.

It took some years for Trinity to be repaired after the Civil War. In 1885 the building was ravaged by a major hurricane, and the next year it was damaged by the great earthquake. By the end of the century, the structural integrity of the building was in doubt. It was pulled down, and a third Trinity sanctuary was built in 1902.

In 1926 Trinity purchased its present church on Meeting Street. The grandly scaled structure, built 1848–1850 for Westminster Presbyterian Church, was designed by Edward C. Jones along Roman Revival lines inspired by the Church of the Madeleine in Paris. The impressive, colossal Corinthian columns of its portico are echoed by paired columns flanking the ornate apse inside the sanctuary.

Trinity's Meeting Street inaugural service took place on February 5, 1928. An educational building, a gift from Mr. and Mrs. Thomas W. Carroll, was added in 1938. In 1957 the congregation bought the lots between its building and Society Street and had them cleared and landscaped. The same year, all of Trinity was refurbished.

When Hurricane Hugo crashed through Charleston on September 21–22, 1989, it left Trinity with serious, but not major, damage. Fortunately, the stained-glass window, created in the Tiffany workshop in New York and brought from the Hasell Street church, was unscathed by the storm. After renovations both inside and out, the congregation celebrated the rededication of Trinity on December 16, 1990.

Bethel United Methodist Church
57 Pitt Street

In 1793 the expanding congregation of Cumberland Street Methodist Church purchased a lot at the corner of Pitt and Boundary

(Calhoun) streets. The lot was used as a cemetery until 1797, when a new church was built on the site. In his journal, Bishop Francis Asbury wrote, "the name of the house shall be Bethel, the Hebrew word for the house of God."

The first Bethel sanctuary was a simple, rectangular meeting house built of wood. In 1853, when a new, larger church was built, the old wooden structure was moved westward on the now enlarged lot and used for class meetings of the black members of Bethel. The biracial nature of the church was retained until 1878. At that time the original church building was donated to the black members; it was moved in 1880 across Calhoun Street to its present site and became Old Bethel. The new Greek Revival sanctuary was designed by "E. Curtis"—probably Ephraim Curtis, a member of a local family of master builders.

During the first half of the nineteenth century, Cumberland and Bethel suffered intermittent persecution because of the Methodists' active education of African American slaves and their perceived antislavery stand. In 1822 there was a crisis when Denmark Vesey, a black

The Bethel United Methodist Church sanctuary

class leader at Bethel, was arrested for inciting rebellion among the slaves. Vesey was hanged for his activities, and the Charleston Methodists distanced themselves from any pro-abolition ideas.

Since it was beyond the range of the Federal bombardment, Bethel was the only Methodist church in the city to remain open throughout the Civil War. During the military occupation following the war, Bethel's congregation managed to retain ownership of the church. The building suffered from neglect during the lean Reconstruction years. In August 1886, a disastrous earthquake damaged it. In 1886–1887 Bethel underwent a major renovation: an organ alcove was added behind the chancel; stained-glass windows were installed; and the galleries, which had been built for the black congregation, were removed. After a hurricane in 1893 prompted further repairs, a coved ceiling of pressed tin was placed in the sanctuary. Shortly afterward, the unusual stenciling along the interior walls was added. The stenciled details have been renewed each time the sanctuary has been repainted.

Interior of St. James United Methodist Church

St. James United Methodist Church
68 Spring Street

In 1791 William Hammet and a group of dissenters from Cumberland Street Methodist Church founded Trinity Primitive Methodist Church. Within a few years, Hammet decided it was time to expand. On January 1, 1795, work began on a second Primitive Methodist church, located beyond the city limits, on King Street just south of Line Street. In his baptismal register at Trinity, Hammet noted that on October 25, 1795, "the new chapel was consecrated & called 'St. James's Chapel,' as he was the great Apostle of practical piety."

The chapel was small and unpretentious, but by 1796 it had its own burial ground. Along with Trinity, St. James petitioned the Methodist Episcopal Church for admission. Admission was awarded both churches in 1816.

When a larger sanctuary was needed, property was purchased at the northwest corner of Spring and Coming Streets. The cornerstone of the church was laid on June 24, 1856. The architect of the new St. James was Louis J. Barbot of the partnership of Barbot & Seyle. Barbot produced a bold Roman Revival building in the Corinthian order, patterned after the temple of Jupiter in Rome. Originally the front stairs were to be a grand direct axial approach 40 feet wide, but the restrictive corner site necessitated breaking the stairway into two perpendicular sections. The change only increased the monumental impression presented by the building.

Beginning in 1862, the Confederate forces in Charleston used St. James as a medical storehouse. When Charleston was evacuated before the Union army took the city, St. James, with Charleston's other Methodist churches, was turned over to the Reverend T. Willard Lewis of the Northern Methodist Church. He assigned St. James to a congregation of black Methodists who used the building until February, 1868, when it was returned to its original membership. In 1946 the South Carolina Methodist Conference officially reinstated the name St. James to the church, which had for years been known as the Spring Street Church.

Sometime during 1953 an antique chandelier that was considered dangerous was removed, and the sanctuary ceiling was repaired. The houses at 70 and 72 Spring Street were bought and demolished to create a parking lot in 1964–1965. On the night of September 21, 1989, Hurricane Hugo passed through Charleston and left St. James heavily damaged. The roof was torn off of the sanctuary and the interior was ruined from the subsequent rains. After a $300,000 renovation, the church was rededicated on November 11, 1990.

Old Bethel United Methodist Church
222 Calhoun Street

In 1793, when the people of Cumberland Street Methodist Church had grown strong enough to contemplate expansion, they purchased a lot at the corner of Pitt and Boundary (Calhoun) Streets. The new church was not begun on the site, however, until 1797. The first Bethel Church was dedicated in 1798, though it was not completed until 1808. At the time of its dedication there was not yet a pulpit or a sounding board (a wooden canopy over the pulpit to help project the speaker's voice into the congregation), and the walls had not been plastered. Old Bethel was the third Methodist

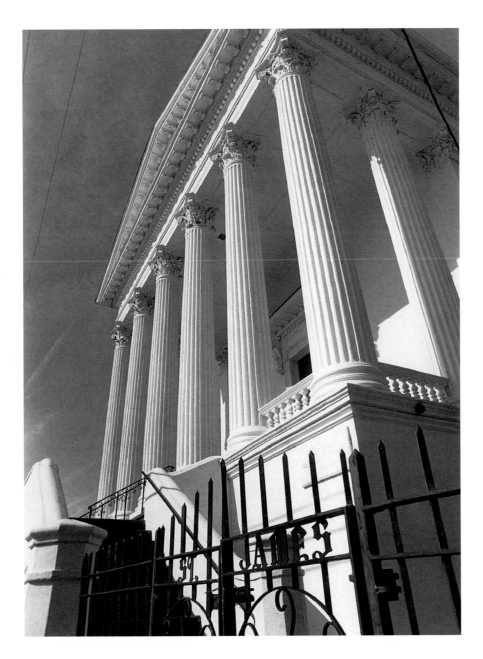

St. James United Methodist Church at Spring and Coming Streets

church to be built in Charleston, following Cumberland and Trinity. After two moves, the sanctuary stands today on Calhoun Street.

In 1817 there were approximately six thousand black Methodists in Charleston. Most of them worshiped at Bethel. (Morris Brown, a free black local preacher, came from this congregation to go secretly to Philadelphia, where he was ordained into the new African Methodist Episcopal Church.) That year there was a confrontation between the white and black class leaders of Bethel. At question was whether the white leaders or the black leaders would control the funds and organization of the black classes. When the white leaders insisted on total authority, the black members walked out en masse. With Brown as their pastor, the blacks formed Charleston's first A.M.E. congregation.

A prominent member of the new A.M.E. church, Denmark Vesey had also been a class leader in Bethel. Vesey used his persuasive teaching of Moses and Exodus to encourage African Americans to rise against their white masters. Rumors of his activities leaked out and Vesey was arrested in June 1822. He and five co-conspirators were hanged on July 2, 1822. The A.M.E. congregation was disbanded forcibly and its building dismantled. Many of the black congregants returned to Bethel. Charleston Methodists, especially those at Bethel, remained suspect for educating slaves and possibly encouraging insurrection.

To make way for a new, larger Bethel sanctuary, the old wooden building was moved to the west side of the lot in 1852 and used only for black class meetings. The white members donated the old sanctuary to the black congregation in 1876. In 1880 it was moved across Calhoun Street and named Old Bethel Methodist Church.

Apart from necessary repairs, Old Bethel has remained much the same through the years. It has a traditional meeting-house style common among dissenting groups. After it was moved across Calhoun Street to its final location, the columned portico and a pentagonal apse were added. In

1919 a pipe organ was installed. The pulpit in use today is the same one from which Bishop Francis Asbury preached when the church was newly opened in 1798.

T*he sanctuary of Old Bethel, the third-oldest Church Structure in Charleston*

Centenary United Methodist Church
60 Wentworth Street

When the Civil War ended, Charleston Methodists encouraged black members to return to their old church rather than join the African Methodist Episcopal (A.M.E.) or Northern Methodist churches. A meeting took place in 1865 between the white leaders of Trinity Methodist Episcopal Church, South, and its black

Old Bethel's pulpit

members. The two groups gathered in Trinity, where the white ministers appealed to the blacks to "Stay with us in your old places in the galleries." In response, the Reverend T. Willard Lewis, a white missionary from the Northern Methodist church, stood and announced, "Brethren and sisters, there will be no galleries in heaven. Those who are willing to go with a church that makes no distinction as to race or color, follow me to the Normal School on the corner of Beaufain and St. Philip's Street." Every black member of Trinity

walked out, and Centenary Methodist was born.

The new congregation needed a new home. With the aid of the Methodist Missionary Society of New England, it entered into negotiations to purchase the Second Baptist Church on Wentworth Street. When the Baptist leaders realized the buyer was a black congregation, they demanded that the $20,000 price be paid in gold. Since gold carried a fifty percent premium, the new requirement meant raising an additional $10,000 in order to buy it through an agent in New York. The gold had to be presented before two o'clock on the afternoon of April 10, 1866, for the contract to close. The gold arrived by train that morning, but the broker refused to accept the bank draft from the northern Missionary Society. The determined Methodists went to George Walton Williams, president of the Carolina Savings Bank and a leader in Trinity Church. Williams knew most of the black leaders well and promptly exchanged their bank draft for cash so the gold could be redeemed. The black leaders presented the two thousand gold double eagles at the appointed place with less than an hour to spare. The congregation took possession of the Wentworth Street sanctuary, rededicated it, and named it Centenary to celebrate the first one hundred years of American Methodism.

The fine Greek Revival structure Centenary bought was designed by Edward Brickell White; its construction began in 1841. The hurricane of August 1911 damaged the building, which was later repaired. In the 1930s, the valuable English pipe organ was rebuilt. The church interior was renovated in 1953, and extensive exterior work was done in 1964. Hurricane Hugo (September 21–22, 1989) inflicted substantial damage on Centenary. After insurance settlements were completed, both the fellowship hall and the sanctuary were restored.

Centenary United Methodist Church on Wentworth Street, originally Second Baptist Church

Grant to those who labor in this place such measures of thy grace and wisdom, that they may neglect no portion of their manifold heritage.

Dedication for the Gabriel Kney Organ,
Cathedral of St. Luke and St. Paul, 1976

NINE
Episcopal Churches
Founded in the Nineteenth Century

Disestablishment of the Church of England following the American Revolution presented an intricacy of legislative and theoretical possibilities. There were twenty established parish churches and at least ninety dissenting congregations. While addressing the issue of separation of Church and State, Charlestonians of the Anglican faith continued to venerate British cultural achievements as they dealt with the advancement of democratic ideals. Christopher Gadsden, the Rutledges, the Draytons, the Middletons, and the Pinckneys were all educated in London or Oxford. Although some would have preferred to continue under the Crown and the Church of England, many of Charleston's most prominent citizens were Anglican and patriot, leading the way on the national level as well as locally.

As the Church of England could not depend upon unified support in Charleston, neither could it count on cooperation in the outlying parishes. As the British armies burned homes and churches containing unauthorized translations of the Psalms (indicating a dissenting Whig interest), they created new opposition among a population that might have otherwise supported the British.

Mobilized by the Baptists, a petition to the legislature to disestablish the Anglican Church was prepared by the Reverend William Tennent, minister of the Congregational Church. William Henry Drayton, former vestryman of St. Andrew's Church and chief justice of South Carolina, assisted and paid for the printing of Tennent's petition, which argued that non-Anglicans were the greater number of citizens and should not be taxed without their consent and that "all good and healthy subjects of the state" ought to be entitled to "free and equal liberty in religious matters." It was to Tennent's and Drayton's credit that the traditional Baptist argument was cast in terms that even many Anglicans could accept. The Dissenters' Petition was introduced in the legislature in 1777 by Christopher Gadsden and supported by Charles Cotesworth Pinckney, also an Anglican. At least half of the members of the Church of England in the assembly were in support of disestablishment.

The interior of St. Luke and St. Paul, renovated after damages from Hurricane Hugo in 1989

The Reverend Edward Jenkins, former rector of St. Bartholomew's in Colleton County and pastor of St. Michael's during the British occupation, was forced to leave when the British evacuated Charles Towne in 1782. By 1784 the Reverend Robert Smith had returned to St. Philip's, and the Church of England became Protestant Episcopal. An initial action toward the appointment of delegates to a Philadelphia convention came in the form of a circular from Dr. William Smith presented to a joint meeting of the vestries of St. Philip's and St. Michael's churches, and delegates were elected in 1785.

In 1790, under the leadership of Governor Charles Pinckney, a new state constitution finalized the complete separation of Church and State in South Carolina. The next year, St. Michael's Church hosted George Washington's visit to Charleston.

On July 4, 1794, at St. Michael's, Dr. David Ramsay delivered an oration, "On the Anniversary of American Independence," endorsing universal equality as "the most effectual method of preserving peace among contending sects." He also recognized Church and State as distinct societies, "which can very well subsist without any alliance or dependence on each other." In 1795 a formal organization was established with an elected Episcopal Bishop for South Carolina.

Cathedral of St. Luke and St. Paul
126 Coming Street

The Cathedral of St. Luke and St. Paul was originally known as St. Paul's, Radcliffeborough. Organized as a mission in 1806, the congregation met in the old French Church until their building was erected on land given by Mrs. Lucretia Radcliffe. Designed by the architects James and John Gordon, it was completed in 1815. It was consecrated in 1816 by Bishop Theodore Dehon, the third Bishop of South Carolina. This was the first Episcopal church in the area to be formally consecrated by an American bishop.

The Cathedral of St. Luke and St. Paul on Coming Street

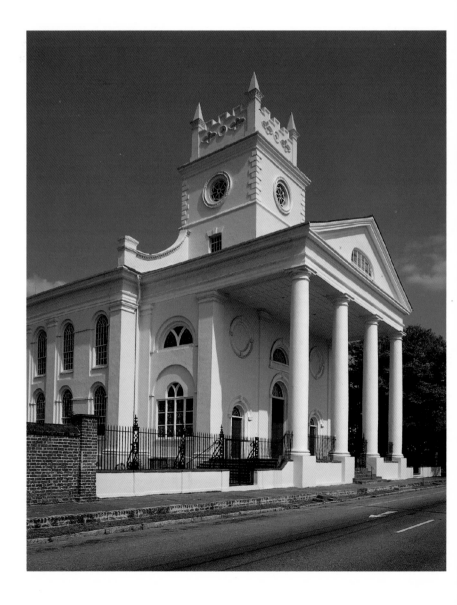

The building was in continuous use during the Civil War, harboring congregations from St. Philip's and St. Michael's, whose churches were closed because of the bombardment by Union cannon nearby. The Reverend Dr. W. B. W. Howe, later Bishop of the Diocese of South Carolina, ministered to these congregations until he was banished for refusing to pray for the President of the United States.

In 1949 St. Paul's merged with Radcliffeborough St. Luke's, on Charlotte Street. Later the building was designated the Cathedral Church for the Diocese of South Carolina, and Bishop Grey Temple was officially enthroned there in 1963. The Cathedral has its own coat of arms, designed by Col. Harry Downing Temple, noted American herald.

The Regency interpretation of the architecture is similar to that of Second Presbyterian Church, also designed by the Gordon brothers. Neither of the churches has its intended steeple. In the case of St. Luke and St. Paul, the load of the original tower was too heavy for the main walls, requiring that the upper tower be dismantled. A lighter Gothic-Revival-style parapet, crenelated with pinnacles, was added, lending an interesting contrast to the Classical Revival style of the building below.

The interior of the cathedral also reflects the Regency style, with woodwork embellished with the sunburst motif, and repeating the sunburst design on the bull's-eye false windows of the tower. Dalcho describes the chancel as "richly painted, and ornamented with Corinthian pilasters having gilt capitals." This description was followed in the 1990 restoration of the interior following the destruction wrought by the hurricane of September 1989. During this restoration an architectural surveyor was hired to ascertain the colors used in the past, and the original color scheme was reinstated. New stained-glass windows, influenced by the style of Christopher Wren's design for St. Paul's, London, were commissioned from the Willett Studios of Philadelphia.

St. Stephen's Episcopal Church, in Ansonborough

St. Stephen's Episcopal Church
67 Anson Street

St. Stephen's Episcopal Church in downtown Charleston dates to the early nineteenth century. Organized by the Charleston Female Domestic Missionary Society in 1822, it was the first "free church" in Episcopal history, a place where one could worship without paying pew rent. The cornerstone for the church buildings was laid on St. Stephen's Day 1835. The new church was consecrated on November 24, 1836.

Until it became an organized mission in 1974, St. Stephen's was considered an unorganized mission, not in union with the Diocesan Convention. As the oldest missionary church in the Diocese of South Carolina, it has had to struggle to cope with the adversities imposed on the Ansonborough community by both natural forces and an economically changing neighborhood.

In 1923 the minister and entire congrega-

The sanctuary of St.
Stephen's Episcopal
Church

The pinnacled spire of
Grace Episcopal Church

tion of Mount Moriah Union Methodist Church joined the Episcopal Church and were given St. Stephen's as their place of worship. The all-black congregation continued to worship there for some sixty-five years. In July 1987 a small number of whites joined St. Stephen's. Old and new members then began a dialogue about what they might do to make this unique church a place for integrated worship. The Reverend A. Houghton was appointed priest-in-charge and has developed St. Stephen's into a church of the people, with the laity making policy and decisions. The words emblazoned over the church doorway, "My house shall be called a house of prayer for all people," became the mission statement for the congregation.

Grace Episcopal Church
98 Wentworth Street

Grace Episcopal Church was founded in 1846 with the intention of establishing an Episcopal church in the growing area of Harleston Village. Initial worship services were held together with the congregation in the chapel at the College of Charleston while the new church was being built.

The building was designed in the Gothic Revival style by Edward Brickell White and completed on November 1, 1848. The pinnacled spire and elaborate stone folds around the great front door are characteristic of this popular style. The interior vaulting is also notable.

The memorial windows of Grace Church are teaching windows, each containing scenes from the life of Christ as well as representations of clergy and laypersons associated with the church. The altar window, the great rear window, four windows in the nave, two in the narthex, and twelve clerestory windows were all designed by the sixth rector, Dr. Ralph Sadler Meadowcroft. Located over the rear doorway, the largest window took over a year to complete. It contains more than ten thousand pieces of glass. A small window on the Epistle side of the

The Gothic-Revival sanctuary of Grace Episcopal,
renovated after damage from Hurricane Hugo

The Church of the Holy Communion at Ashley and Cannon

narthex contains an angel with the face of a small girl who drowned on Sullivan's Island.

Grace Church was closed for a year in 1864 because of bombardment from Morris Island. The church was reopened soon after the evacuation, during Federal occupation.

Church of the Holy Communion
218 Ashley Avenue

The Church of the Holy Communion was founded in 1848, and its present building was consecrated in 1855. Since its construction, the building has undergone two expansions. The rear wall was removed in 1868, and a recessed chancel and organ chamber were built to accommodate a new organ, stained-glass windows, and a marble altar with memorial cross. The present chancel was constructed when the rear of the building was again removed in 1871. Transepts were added at that time, and the roof was raised and replaced with a new roof modeled

Holy Communion's marble pulpit and unique sounding board

after that of Trinity Hall in Cambridge, England. Additional stained-glass windows were also added. Since 1872 the church's interior appearance has been unchanged.

The Reverend Anthony Toomer Porter became rector of the Church of the Holy Communion in 1854. He revived the practice of wearing eucharistic vestments according to the church calendar and using colored altar hangings. Dr. Porter also used traditional liturgical elements in the worship services to reestablish the Anglican form, an emphasis that is still characteristic of this parish.

The interior of the Church of the Holy Communion, with its arched mahogany hammer-beam ceiling, is rich in Christian symbols.

St. Mark's Episcopal Church
Thomas and Warren

St. Mark's Episcopal Church was organized in 1865 as an independent parish by a group of prominent black Episcopalians who found themselves without a place to worship at the end of the Civil War. The city gave them the use of the Orphan's Chapel on Vanderhorst Street. The Reverend J. Mercier Green and the Reverend Joseph Seabrook, both from Grace Episcopal Church, served as co-pastors, alternating Sundays to hold services for the new congregation.

The congregation gathered at various locations before purchasing the site of the present church in 1875. St. Mark's was designed by Louis J. Barbot and built by the Devereaux Brothers. The building was completed in 1878. The Reverend A. Toomer Porter was pastor for ten years, from the time the church was erected until it had the second-largest membership of any church in the diocese. After becoming Dr. Porter's assistant minister at St. Mark's in 1887, the Reverend John Henry Mingo Pollard became St. Mark's first black rector. Dr. Pollard also ministered to Calvary Church and was involved in starting the missions of St. Stephen's in Charleston, Epiphany in Summerville, and St. Andrew's.

From 1875 to 1885 St. Mark's sought unsuccessfully to become a participant in the annual Convention of the Diocese of South Carolina. Neither the influence of the Bishop nor the clergy could overcome the prejudice of the time. Dr. Pollard resigned in 1898 to become Archdeacon in the Diocese of North Carolina, but the church struggled on. The place of black Episcopalians in the Convention continued to be an issue, full participation being denied St. Mark's again in 1915. In the face of competition from other denominations that gave more support to their black congregations, membership began a decline that has continued to the present. Numerous dedicated clergy have struggled to keep the congregation alive during

A view of St. Mark's sanctuary showing the mahogany arch and reredos above the chancel

difficult times. Strong lay leadership can be credited with preserving St. Mark's during periods without a pastor. In 1965, one hundred years after its founding, St. Mark's formally became a part of the Convention of the Diocese of South Carolina.

A classic temple form, the design of St. Mark's shows the continuing interest in the Greek Revival style following the Civil War. The roof of the structure has been replaced twice—after storms in 1885 and 1989. Many improvements were made to the interior after the 1989 hurricane, including a stained-glass window over the altar, recreated from a photograph of the original window. St. Mark's 125th anniversary was celebrated in 1990.

St. Paul's Episcopal Church, Summerville
316 West Carolina Avenue

St. Paul's, Summerville, began in the early 1800s as a summer church on a pineland ridge used by the city residents as a retreat from the malaria of the low-lying plantations. The village of Summerville drew from the neighboring parishes of St. James Goose Creek; St. George, Dorchester; St. Andrew's; and St. Paul's, Stono.

The Reverend Philip Gadsden, rector of St. Paul's, Stono, ministered to both churches. The first church was built on a site near the present building and consecrated in 1832. In 1836 the new church became a chapel of ease to the parish church of St. Paul's, Stono.

The congregation incorporated as St. Paul's Episcopal Church, Summerville, in 1855. In 1856 the present church building was completed. The church remained a chapel of ease under the vestry of St. Paul's, Stono, until after the Civil War. It became independent in 1866 when admitted in union with the Convention as St. Paul's Church in St. George's Parish. In 1875 the earlier name, St. Paul's, Summerville, was reinstated.

In 1877 the church was enlarged and the stained-glass window behind the altar added. The earthquake of 1886 caused considerable damage to the building, prompting the installation of earthquake rods. Additions to the rear of the building were made during the earlier part of this century, and extensive restoration was completed in 1986. Of note is the 1500-pipe Tracker organ installed in 1988.

Christ St. Paul's Church, Adams Run

Christ St. Paul's Church at Adams Run, constructed on the present site after the great earthquake of 1886, has an interesting history dating from 1836. Built on the site of an early eighteenth-century Presbyterian church in the village of Wilton, the original Christ Church was described by a contemporary observer as "a beautiful specimen of chaste and simple Grecian architecture." It served a population whose ancestors had been among the earlier settlers of the Carolina colony, having founded Wilton (or New London as it was originally known) before 1683.

Like many other public and private structures, Christ St. Paul's Church suffered ill use

St. Paul's Episcopal Church, Summerville

The interior of Christ St. Paul's Church, Adams Run

Interior view of St. Andrew's Episcopal

during the Civil War. The end of the conflict found it a shuttered derelict, a church with a scattered congregation; the shift of population during and after Reconstruction left the old church isolated from its people. In 1881 plans were made to build a new sanctuary in the nearby village of Adams Run. Rather than abandon the old building, the congregation dismantled it in 1887 and moved it to the new site, where it was reconstructed, using most of the original materials. A recessed chancel with a triple window was added in 1911, and the present parish house was constructed in 1930.

In 1960 Christ Church Parish merged with St. Paul's Meggett to become Christ St. Paul's Church Parish

St. Andrew's Episcopal Church, Mount Pleasant
440 Whilden St.

St. Andrew's, six miles south of Christ Episcopal Church, was organized in 1835 as a chapel of ease. A frame building was built on Whilden Street in that year and consecrated as St. Andrew's Chapel. This building was later sold to the Masonic Order of Mount Pleasant.

St. Andrew's Episcopal Church, set among oak trees in old Mount Pleasant

Grace Chapel, Rockville

The present structure, erected in 1857 on Whilden Street in the village of Mount Pleasant, was constructed in a vernacular neo-Gothic style.

The chapel maintained ties with Christ Church during the Civil War. After the war, St. Andrew's helped raise money for a restoration of Christ Church and consequently received the old altar from the mother church.

The earthquake of 1886 damaged the chapel and rectory. Five hundred dollars covered the repairs. The rectory burned in 1907 and was immediately rebuilt. The congregations of St. Andrew's and Christ Church separated in 1954, when St. Andrew's became a parish church.

Grace Chapel, Rockville, Wadmalaw Island
Maybank Highway

Grace Chapel is situated amid moss-draped live oaks along Maybank Highway in Rockville. It was built c. 1840 as a chapel of ease to St. John's Episcopal Church on Johns Island. In 1885 Grace Chapel was moved on palmetto logs to its present location from its original, more central, lot.

Built in the Greek Revival style, the church

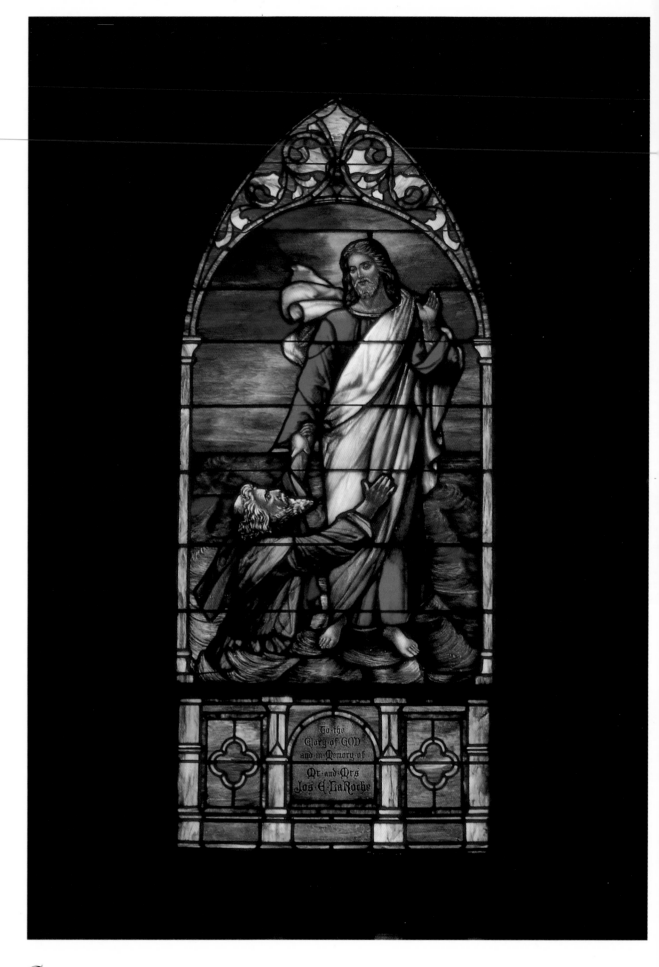

Grace Chapel's Tiffany window

was restored in 1897 following the 1893 hurricane. Lightning damaged the cupola and cross in 1929. The tower bell was later mounted outside the chapel for use as a fire bell for the village.

The chapel entrance introduces a stained-glass window that was discovered to be a signed Tiffany when it was cleaned in the early 1980s. This window matches one in the church at the U.S. Naval Academy in Annapolis, Maryland.

Other treasures contained within Grace Chapel include an elegant handmade copper cross, pine tongue-in-groove woodwork, hand-blown panes of glass, and a Bible given to the church in 1862 by a Confederate soldier. The pews and kneeling benches are original to the chapel, as is the old pump organ.

St. James Santee Chapel
McClellanville

St. James, McClellanville, was consecrated by Bishop Howe on November 2, 1890. Built for the use of planters who spent their summers in the town of McClellanville, St. James was a chapel of ease for the parish of old St. James Santee Parish Church. After 1870, as most of the congregation set up residence near McClellanville, the life of the parish eventually centered around the chapel. St. James, McClellanville, came into year-round use beginning in 1912.

Both the interior and the exterior of St. James Chapel display noteworthy wood carving by A. H. Lucas. A winsome example of Carpenter Gothic, St. James's style is matched by that of Bethel A.M.E. in McClellanville, a similar structure possibly done by the same hand. An altar cross and memorial window were installed in memory of Lucas in 1938.

Hurricane Hugo (1989) was not the first to take its toll on McClellanville. The Reverend H. M. Jarvis, a former rector, described a baptism "in the midst of the great storm of August, 1893, while the rain was beating heavily upon the windows, several feet of salt water capped by the roaring waves surrounding the church, and the fierce tempest unceasingly thundering its threatenings." For over a hundred years, St. James has never ceased to bear witness to the faith of its congregation.

Cypress-shingled
St. James Santee Chapel
in McClellanville

H*and-carved Victorian screens adorn the sanctuary*
of St. James Santee Chapel.

To provide for ourselves a house to meet in for religious worship agreeable to our desires, according to the light of God.

Bishop Richard Allen, 1794

TEN
African Methodist Episcopal

The African Methodist Episcopal Church in the United States had its beginnings in 1787 when Richard Allen, refusing to be further victimized by racial segregation, broke from St. George's Methodist Church in Philadelphia and founded the Free African Society, adhering to the doctrines of Methodism established in the 1700s by John Wesley. The African Methodist Episcopal Church was organized in 1816, with Allen as its first bishop.

In 1791 an organization similar to the Free African Society was formed in Charleston under the Reverend Morris Brown, a free black preacher affiliated with the congregation at Bethel Methodist Church. Brown had secretly traveled to Philadelphia, where he was ordained into the new Free African Society. He then returned to Charleston to join with other black ministers and laymen to secede from the Methodist Church and become affiliated with the Free African Society in Philadelphia.

The three churches that formed under the Free African Society in Charleston were renamed the Bethel Circuit. They were located in the suburbs of Ansonborough, Hampstead, and Cow Alley, now known as Philadelphia Alley, in the French Quarter of Charleston.

Emanuel African Methodist Episcopal Church was founded by Brown, its congregation emerging from the Hampstead Free African Church. Brown later became the second bishop of the African Methodist Episcopal Church.

The sanctuary of Emmanuel A.M.E. Church

Emanuel A.M.E. Church
110 Calhoun Street

Emanuel A.M.E. rose from the Hampstead congregation of the Bethel Circuit, located at Reid and Hanover streets. By 1818 it had a membership of about one thousand members. In 1822 Denmark Vesey, a carpenter who had

E*manuel A.M.E Church on Calhoun Street,*
the oldest of this denomination in the South

bought himself out of slavery, laid plans in the Hampstead church for an insurrection. Word of the rebellion leaked out, Vesey and some of his followers were executed, and the Hampstead church was burned by white citizens. Morris Brown was not implicated but, because of bad feelings engendered by the insurrection, went to Philadelphia. By 1834 all black churches were closed by the state legislature.

In the years following, some Bethel Circuit members returned to white churches, and others continued the tradition of the African church by worshiping underground. The continuation of meetings of the Hampstead congregation enabled them to resurface in 1865, three thousand strong.

In 1865 the Bethel Circuit purchased the present site of Emanuel. This site was most appealing because of its location. It was north of Boundary Street (now Calhoun), where blacks could live and worship more freely. Bishop Daniel Payne, who had been forced to leave Charleston in 1835 because of his connection with a black school on Tradd Street that was outlawed by the state, returned now to reorganize the congregation. The Reverend Richard H. Cain, who later became a United States congressman, was assigned as the pastor, and the church was renamed Emanuel, meaning "God with us."

A wooden two-story structure was built in 1872 and then destroyed by the earthquake of 1886. The present brick structure was completed in 1891. The bodies of the Reverend Rufin Nichols, who led the building effort, and his wife were exhumed and entombed in the steeple. The towering Charleston green top of this steeple was destroyed by Hurricane Hugo in 1989 but was rebuilt the following year.

The sanctuary of Emanuel still contains the wooden pews, altar, and chandeliers of 1891. The present massive pipe organ was dedicated in 1908. The gas lamps of days past have been preserved and line the sides of the church beneath the balcony railings. The arched ceiling contains intricate patterns of design. Two mu-

rals of Christ appear on either side of the altar, separated by a huge stained-glass window. The sanctuary seats 2,500, giving the church the largest seating capacity of Charleston's African-American congregations.

Morris Brown A.M.E. Church
13 Morris Street

Morris Brown African Methodist Episcopal Church was born out of the congregation at Emanuel A.M.E. Church when, in 1867, a few members withdrew to establish a new church. The African Methodist Church had been growing rapidly in South Carolina as well as elsewhere on the Eastern seaboard and through the South, especially after the conclusion of the Civil War. The formation of new congregations, therefore, was inevitable.

The group from Emanuel secured its first pastor, the Reverend Richard H. Cain, in 1873. He rented a hall at 13 Morris Street once used by soldiers as a meeting place. In the few years that followed, the lot was purchased, the hall was moved to the back of it, and a chapel was built in front.

The church was named after the Reverend Morris Brown, who was famous for leading the movement in Charleston to organize black Methodists at the beginning of the 1800s. After leaving Charleston for Philadelphia because of the feelings engendered by the Denmark Vesey affair in 1822, he was consecrated the second bishop of the A.M.E. denomination in 1828 and was the only A.M.E. bishop in America from 1831 to 1836. Bishop Brown died in 1849, having been stricken with paralysis five years earlier while attending a conference in Canada. He never lived to see the permanent organization of the church he had started.

Besides its namesake, Morris Brown A.M.E. includes in its history other important names. The Reverend Daniel Payne was the third pastor and known as a great educator. The Reverend Dr. B. J. Glover, pastor from 1950 to 1953, went on to become president of Allen

Colorful murals depicting the story of Moses adorn
the interior of Morris Brown A.M.E. Church.

Morris Brown A.M.E. Church

University in Atlanta. The Reverend Cain, first
pastor, the Reverend M. B. Salters, and the
Reverend W. W. Beckett all became bishops in
the A.M.E. denomination.

The original wooden structure at Morris
Brown A.M.E. was eventually widened. Starting
in 1953 the church was renovated further and
brick veneer was added. As it stands today, it still
contains elements of the original chapel. The interior is finished in a Neoclassical style.

Mt. Zion A.M.E. Church
5 Glebe Street

The congregation of the present-day Mt. Zion
A.M.E. Church arose from the overcrowding
at Emanuel A.M.E. Church on Calhoun
Street. In 1881 one group at Emanuel favored
building an entirely new structure, but another favored repairing the old building. The
final solution was for all to work together in
the remodeling of Emanuel. The second

group then purchased another building.

In 1882 it happened that the building of Central Presbyterian Church on Meeting Street (later known as Westminster Presbyterian Church and now Trinity Methodist Church) and the building of the Zion Presbyterian Church on Glebe Street were both offered for sale. The two churches planned to merge, and their strategy was that one building would be sold to whoever offered the nearest amount to the price set for it when they were put up for auction. No offer was received for the Meeting Street building, but $15,000 was offered for the

Zion Presbyterian Church building by the group from Emanuel A.M.E., who became its buyers. The name Zion was retained and the church became Mt. Zion A.M.E. Church in 1882.

The lot upon which the church stands was originally a part of the glebe land attached to St. Michael's and St. Philip's Episcopal Churches and divided between them in 1797. In 1847 the lot was leased to Glebe Street Presbyterian Church, which built its church on it that year. In 1856 it was purchased in fee-simple, then in 1866 was sold to Zion Presbyterian. Zion and Glebe Street Presbyterian Churches merged, re-

*S*anctuary of Mt.
Zion A.M.E. Church

tained the name Zion, and in 1882 merged with Central Presbyterian Church on Meeting Street to form what became Westminster Presbyterian.

Mt. Zion A.M.E. Church was damaged by fire in 1937. Repairs were made promptly and services resumed in 1938. The essential structure, reminiscent of the early simplicity of Presbyterian churches, was preserved. The design has been attributed to Francis D. Lee, a Charleston architect, and it reflects the influence of Sir John Soane, a prominent English architect of the late eighteenth and early nineteenth centuries whose designs were published and often adapted.

ELEVEN
Unitarian - Universalist

The prototype of religious freedom initiated by the pastorate of William Tennent and the early Dissenters was incorporated into the Archdale Street Church when the new structure was built to accommodate the expanding Meeting Street congregation. The Meeting and Archdale Street churches constituted a single corporate body until 1817, when the Archdale congregation broke away to follow the Reverend Anthony Forster. This congregation received the Archdale Street property in settlement with the Independent Church, becoming the Second Independent Church of Charleston.

The Reverend Samuel Gilman, a pre-Emersonian, rationalist Unitarian from Harvard, ministered the church from 1819 until 1859. Despite the political differences between Northerners and Southerners at this time, Gilman's expansive personality and broad-minded disposition made him a natural civic leader. He established relationships with other religious groups, drawing audiences many times the size of his own church's membership. It is noteworthy that through Gilman's friendship with Isaac Harby and Beth Elohim, he is credited with being a catalyst in the development of Reform Judaism in Charleston.

The American Unitarian Association was organized in 1825, and a new charter was granted in 1839 to change the name of the Second Independent Church to the Unitarian Church of Charleston. A merger of the American Unitarian and Universalist denominations in 1962 resulted in the creation of the Unitarian-Universalist Association, with which this church became affiliated.

Detail of the fanned ceiling that graces the sanctuary at the Unitarian Church of Charleston

Unitarian Church
8 Archdale Street

The church at 8 Archdale Street is the oldest Unitarian church in the South. The original structure on the site was begun in 1772 to serve the expanding congregation of the Independent Church (the Old White Meeting), which stood on the site of the present Circular Congregational Church at 150 Meeting Street.

During the siege of Charleston in the Revolutionary War, a British shell burst in the

T*he Unitarian Church of Charleston was the first of its denomination in the South.*

churchyard while services were going on in the uncompleted sanctuary. As a result, according to an early-nineteenth-century source, "the worshipers immediately dispersed, and assembled no more until happier times." While the British occupied the city, from 1780 to 1783, work on the structure stopped. The church building was used during this time for stabling horses, among other things. Construction resumed after the war, and the church was at last dedicated in October 1787.

In 1817 the Archdale Street congregation formally became Unitarian when it was chartered as the Second Independent Church of Charleston, South Carolina. Two years later, the Reverend Samuel Gilman, a native of New England and a Harvard graduate who is credited as the composer of "Fair Harvard," began his thirty-nine-year ministry at the church.

The present church was created by reconstructing, refining, and expanding the earlier building, between 1852 and 1854. Under the direction of Francis D. Lee, a partner in the Charleston architectural firm of Jones and Lee, a grand structure in the perpendicular neo-Gothic style was superimposed upon the shell of the old Georgian church. As Gilman saw it, "This retention, as far as possible, of the old structure, was due to a natural regard and respect for time-honored associations, rather than to any considerations of mere economy, for the cost of an entirely new edifice would scarcely have exceeded the repairs introduced and perfected, augmented as these have been by the difficulties surmounted in perforating the faithful old masonry to admit the new and lofty windows, and of compassing the ancient massive tower to build one far more lofty and imposing."

When the congregation finally moved into the new sanctuary on April 2, 1854, it found a remarkably different church within the old walls, one which the *Charleston Daily Standard* described as having been "completed in a style of great magnificence." And, as the *Standard* added approvingly, it was "already paid for."

Among many architectural refinements, the grand Gothic tower and sturdy buttresses are the most obvious external evidence of the re-

design of the eighteenth-century structure. But it is on the interior that Lee left his most dramatic stamp. There he created a dazzling display of peaked windows, soaring Gothic columns, and delicate tracery which together draw the eye upward to highly ornamented fan-vaulted ceilings, the design of which was based on Henry VII's chapel at Westminster Abbey. In deference to the need to combine the modern with the traditional, the architect also specified that the entire church be illuminated by gas lamps.

In his sermon of dedication the Reverend Gilman spoke of a "far distant day, when the traces of decaying age shall be discerned around thy buttresses and mouldings, and pinnacles, and spires." But in that day, he said, a visitor might look on the structure and say, "There stands the pile from which nought but good influences have ever proceeded . . . which has faithfully ministered heavenly and earthly blessings to generations as they have glided past."

With the coming of the Civil War less than a decade after completion of the renovation, it seemed that the "distant day" Gilman had described might be at hand. But as bad as the situation became, the worst was avoided. The building itself survived the war, though its congregation was scattered and its records and furnishings—which had been evacuated for safekeeping—were lost in the destruction of the city of Columbia in 1865.

In 1886 the church was severely damaged by the disastrous earthquake which struck Charleston, and members of the congregation feared for a time that it might not be possible to save the structure. Fortunately, with the aid of Unitarians all over the country who contributed to its rebuilding, it was largely restored to its previous grandeur. An 1854 picture of the church shows some Gothic embellishments which are no longer extant, having apparently been lost in the earthquake and not replaced. Still, thanks to the conscientious restoration of the late 1800s, a visitor to the churchyard today will see, not a ruin, but the "venerable walls . . . ye fair and exquisite adornments" which Gilman so eloquently celebrated in 1854.

The Gothic interior of the Unitarian Church of Charleston

TWELVE

Reformed Episcopal

The Reformed Episcopal Church, a national denomination composed primarily of whites in the North and blacks in the South, first set roots in South Carolina and Charleston in 1875, only two years after it originated in New York City. The Reverend George Cummins of New York, who previously had been the Assistant Episcopal Bishop of Kentucky, withdrew from the Protestant Episcopal Church after a major dispute over ritual and doctrine and formed this new denomination.

At the same time in the South, black Episcopalians—now freedmen—were becoming increasingly frustrated with the manner in which they were treated within the Protestant Episcopal Church. Accustomed to liturgical worship and the Book of Common Prayer, these Episcopalians wanted acceptance in the Protestant Episcopal Church and freedom to worship in their new status as freedmen. Experiencing what they considered second-class treatment, they turned toward the Reformed Episcopal Church in the North and pleaded for admission.

It is ironic that the pleas of these black Episcopalians were heard not so much by Northern Reformed Episcopalians as by a Southern-born white Confederate veteran officer by the name of Peter Fayssoux Stevens.

Stevens was a graduate of the Citadel, in Charleston, and was the Confederate colonel who gave the order to fire the first shot of the Civil War. During the war he felt a calling to

H*oly Trinity Reformed Episcopal Church on Bull Street*

the ministry and subsequently was ordained into the Protestant Episcopal Church. Prior to his ministry he helped to educate African Americans. After his ordination he worked exclusively with Episcopal freedmen. When freedmen were no longer invited to the white churches, where as slaves they had sat in the balconies, the Reverend Stevens led them in building roadside chapels that were easily accessible and open to the whole community. In time he founded the Missionary Jurisdiction of the South of the Reformed Episcopal Church and became its first bishop. He also founded the Cummins Theological Seminary in Charleston, now located in Summerville alongside the Southern headquarters of this denomination.

Holy Trinity Reformed Episcopal Church
51 Bull Street

Situated modestly amid the residences of Bull Street, this modified Classical Revival church was the first building of its denomination erected in South Carolina. The church's black membership originally worshiped as part of the congregation at Calvary Protestant Episcopal Church, established for blacks by the Mission Society of the Protestant Episcopal Diocese in South Carolina. However, because the black congregation at Calvary was under the direction of a white deacon and did not own the building, a portion of it withdrew to establish its own church.

This course of action brought the departing group in contention with the authorities of the Protestant Episcopal Church. The group therefore made application on November 18, 1874, for admission to the Reformed Episcopal Church. The Reverend Benjamin Johnson of Georgia, formerly a priest in the Protestant Episcopal Church, was sent to take charge of the work in Charleston. On July 6, 1875, this body of believers was organized under the name Holy Trinity Reformed Episcopal Church.

After worshiping in a variety of locations, the congregation finally erected its own building on Bull Street. Reportedly the builders, carpenters from Charleston, took only three weeks to complete their work. The cornerstone was laid in 1880 by Bishop Peter Fayssoux Stevens. No record has been found of the designer of the church. It may have been Bishop Stevens or the local contractors Welling and Gleason.

A simple wooden structure with a gable roof, the church is fronted by a modified Classical Revival portico. The centered entrance

Holy Trinity Reformed Episcopal, with its coved ceiling and brass chandeliers once lit by gas

and two flanking windows are surmounted by fanlights. The interior has a similar simplicity with a gently coved ceiling and small brass chandeliers, once gas and now electric.

St. Stephen's Reformed Episcopal Church, Summerville
North Palmetto Avenue

St. Stephen's Reformed Episcopal Church in Summerville was begun under the leadership of Bishop Peter Stevens, noted earlier as the extraordinarily dedicated and zealous first bishop of the Reformed Episcopal Church in the Missionary Jurisdiction of the South. Bishop Stevens resided in Charleston but taught at State College in Orangeburg. He often traveled through Summerville and thus became interested in starting a mission in that town.

The church was begun in 1885. It is somewhat typical architecturally of the twenty-seven other

Lowcountry mission churches established by 1887 for emerging denominations of Episcopal freedmen, who were relatively poor farmers.

Bishop Stevens purchased a quarter-block of property in Summerville from the Southern Railway Company. The carpenter who built the church received for his services the corner half of the quarter-block.

It should be noted that inside this quaint church there is a miniature pew for use by children. It was built before special accommodations for children in churches became fashionable.

The sanctuary of St. Stephen's Reformed Episcopal. The carpenter received land for his services to the church.

St. John's Reformed Episcopal Church
91 Anson Street

The church building of St. John's Reformed Episcopal Church on Anson Street, across from the Gaillard Auditorium, is not unlike

St. Stephen's Reformed Episcopal Church, Summerville

The sanctuary of St. John's Reformed Episcopal Church

other historic church buildings in Charleston in that it housed previous congregations. Its history, therefore, is entwined with portions of the history of religious life in Charleston.

Originally the church was erected in 1850 as the Zion Presbyterian Church. In 1861 the building was purchased by the Roman Catholic Church and became St. Joseph's Catholic Church, which it remained for the next century. It served the large Irish Catholic population that had settled about the east end of Calhoun Street and along the Cooper River waterfront. At the time of its organization, St. Joseph's was the fourth Catholic church organized in the city.

St. Joseph's soon encompassed the congregation of another church, St. Paul's, which was dedicated soon after its organization to German-speaking Catholics. Before long its priest left to serve as a chaplain in the Confederate army, and the church closed. Many of St. Paul's members joined St. Joseph's. St. Joseph's later became one of the largest Catholic parishes in the city.

St. Joseph's was badly damaged when it was

St. John's Reformed Episcopal on Anson Street was once St. Joseph's Catholic Church.

Interior view of St. John's sanctuary

*T̲he Georgia pine interior of Bishop Pengelley Memorial Chapel,
Cummins Theological Seminary, Summerville*

struck several times by shells during the Civil War. Some repairs were undertaken in 1867. Later the church was almost completely rebuilt except for the front and side walls. The renovated church had a high, vaulted ceiling, a transept, a rounded apse, and fourteen stained-glass windows. It was dedicated in 1883.

St. John's Reformed Episcopal Church was organized in 1906 just a few blocks away at 43 Elizabeth Street in the home of the Reverend Primus Jefferson. By instruction of Bishop Stevens, Jefferson went in search of a more suitable place for services. After some time he found a building at 48 Calhoun Street known as St. Michael's Hall, formerly the United Engine House. The congregation leased the building for three months. Bishop Stevens then decided to buy the property himself and rent it to the congregation for a small sum.

In 1909 Bishop Stevens resigned from his work because of failing health. He was replaced by Bishop Pengelley, who saw the need for a larger building for the growing congregation. Money was raised locally and in the North, and by 1911 a cornerstone was laid. The church was finished between 1914 and 1923. In 1942, when the city of Charleston expanded East Bay Street from Calhoun to Chapel Street, it moved St. John's Church from 48 to 52 Calhoun Street. The church received a brick veneer in 1959 and continued to stand at the corner of East Bay and Calhoun until the 1980s, at which time it was demolished.

The congregation had begun to search for a new location long before the building came down. In 1969 it discovered the vacant St. Joseph's Church at 91 Anson, a few blocks away. St. Joseph's had closed its doors in 1965 as a result of a sharp decline in membership during the 1950s and '60s. Next to it was a school building that looked like an old wooden church; it had been in use from 1892 until the early 1950s. In 1971, after continued negotiations, the St. John's congregation marched from 52 Calhoun Street to 91 Anson, where it is still located. A year later the church officially opened as St. John's Reformed Episcopal Church. Since that time, only the effects of Hurricane Hugo have been occasion for substantial renovations.

Bishop Pengelley Memorial Chapel, originally St. Barnabas Episcopal Mission in Summerville

Bishop Pengelley Memorial Chapel, Summerville

East 6th South Street

Situated in Summerville's west side, amid azalea bushes just to the rear of the Cummins Theological Seminary of the Reformed Episcopal Church, this old wooden chapel has a history that reaches back to 1884. At that time, the Reverend Guerry, rector of St. Paul's Protestant Episcopal Church in Summerville, decided to establish the St. Barnabas Mission along what is now U.S. Highway 78 on the east side of Summerville. Reportedly the people of this community were descendants of a group of people of diverse ethnicity—Indian, black, and white—from the Ridgeville area to the northwest of Summerville. In this mission a Sunday school was founded, then a day school, and then the chapel itself, completed in 1891 and consecrated by Bishop Capers in 1895.

By 1939 the mission became dormant, and in 1945 the chapel building was sold by the Diocese of South Carolina to Bishop Joseph E. Kearney of the Reformed Episcopal Church for use as the chapel of the Cummins Memorial Theological Seminary. Because the chapel's location on the north side of the Dorchester County Services Building was in the right-of-way for the highway that became U.S. 78, the building was partially disassembled and rolled on logs to a location on the grounds of the seminary at Main and 4th North Street.

The chapel was named in honor of Bishop A. L. Pengelley, the second bishop of the Reformed Episcopal Church in the Missionary Jurisdiction of the South. Bishop Pengelley, a Canadian, provided significant leadership in the years between 1909 and 1922 in buying land in Summerville for the seminary and seminarian residences.

In 1981 the chapel was once again partially dismantled and moved to its present site at East 6th South Street, where it continues its service as the chapel of the Cummins Memorial Theological Seminary. The seminary itself has been relocated to the grounds and buildings of the former Pinewood School.

The lovely wood of the chancel is Georgia curly pine, noted for its intrinsic graining and hardness. The original altar, which stood below the triptych paneling, was remodeled into the pulpit. The original bishop's chair and prayer desk are preserved. The building was constructed in the chapel design of its period and is frequently the subject of artists' paintings and sketches.

THIRTEEN

Praise House

The praise house is a part of the vanishing scene of Southern culture and history. Prior to the Civil War, each plantation had its own praise house or proximity to one. Sometimes it was erected by the plantation owner; other times it was the home of the eldest black spiritual leader on the plantation. Services for the slaves were held by missionaries on an irregular basis, if at all.

The leaders of these plantation groups were persons of considerable authority in spiritual matters. They have been described as direct lineal descendants of the African medicine man. They presided over meetings, weddings, and funerals and provided spiritual advice.

The praise house's most important function was to assist the prospective member in seeking salvation. This involved testing by dreams and visions, followed by instructions in doctrine and church lore and then examination by the praise house committee. If the praise house was also a church, the final step was examination by the church deacons.

Central to praise house activity were the black spirituals, in which prayer, possession, music, and dance were linked in an ancient African affinity. In the Sea Island praise house, all members could and did respond when another member prayed aloud or sang. This is called the shout style. One after another, the island singers added their comments and responses in melody, rhythm, and dance, pouring out rich harmonies and vibrant, complex rhythms. From this tradition came the work songs, blues, and jazz so famous in American music.

T*he praise house*
Moving Star Hall on
Johns Island

The plank benches and potbellied stove of Moving Star Hall (photo by Elias Bull, 1971)

Moving Star Hall, Johns Island
River Road

Moving Star Hall on Johns Island is the best-known example of a Charleston area praise house. Through the years, Moving Star Hall was a central meeting place for local sea islanders and housed a tend-the-sick and burial society, a secret fraternal order, and a community for worship. In its Sunday night worship services, each person would take a turn preaching, testifying, praying, and "raising a song."

Moving Star Hall was built around 1914. As of 1971 it had not been altered. Probably a reconstruction of an earlier praise house, it is a one-room building on a low brick foundation. Its interior is devoid of decoration. The furniture consists of backless benches constructed of a single board. Along one wall is a bench at right angles to the others where deacons sit as judges. At the far end, opposite the entrance, is a slightly raised platform, on top of which are a plain table and a single chair for the teacher. The walls, ceiling, and floor are made of wood. Heat is provided by a potbellied stove.

In 1964 civil rights folksinger Guy Carawan, with financial assistance from the Newport Folk Festival, organized a folk festival on Johns Island. The performers were the singers from Moving Star Hall. The festival was held on an annual basis for several years. These singers later went on to perform at the Coffee House in Los Angeles and the Newport Folk Festival. Their music is still being recorded.

Let every man abide in the same calling wherein he was called.
1 Corinthians 7:20

FOURTEEN

Interdenominational

St. Luke's Chapel at the Medical University of South Carolina is located on grounds that were originally the site of a Federal military arsenal. The property was obtained in 1880 by the trustees of Holy Communion Church Institute and the Reverend Dr. A. Toomer Porter, rector of the Church of the Holy Communion. In 1883 a large gun carriage house was modified for use as a chapel by increasing the height of the walls, raising a Gothic roof, and adding stained-glass windows. It was named St. Timothy's Chapel, and the school became Porter Military Academy (later Porter Gaud School for Boys) in honor of Dr. Porter.

The school moved in 1965, and the chapel became part of the Medical University of South Carolina. In 1966 it was rededicated as the interdenominational Chapel of St. Luke, in honor of St. Luke the physician.

The chapel roof was devastated by Hurricane Hugo in 1989. The storm knocked one wall to the ground and caused extensive damage to the pews and stained-glass windows. Restoration of the building was begun in 1993.

St. Luke's Chapel at the Medical University of South Carolina

The interior of St. Luke's Chapel before its partial destruction by Hurricane Hugo of 1989

FIFTEEN

Greek Orthodox

Holy Trinity Greek
Orthodox Church on
Race Street

In the late 1700s one of the first persons of Greek descent to settle in the New World moved to Charleston. Maria Gracia, the daughter of a Greek merchant from Smyrna, in Asia Minor, had married Dr. Andrew Turnbull, an Englishman, who set out to found a colony near St. Augustine known as New Smyrna. When that settlement failed, the couple moved to Charleston.

The first Greek Orthodox Church service was performed in 1908 at St. John's Episcopal Church, at the corner of Amherst and Hanover Streets. Following that, the Greek Orthodox congregation used a house at the corner of Calhoun and Coming Streets for services.

In 1909 approximately fifty Greeks gathered at 345 King Street, the home of Theodore Papadakos, and organized the Parthenon Society. The following year, the seventy-member Grecian Society of Charleston was formed at a meeting held at Carpenter's Hall on Vanderhorst Street.

The richly ornamented altar at Holy Trinity

Holy Trinity Greek Orthodox Church
30 Race Street

On May 25, 1911, the cornerstone was laid for Charleston's first Greek Orthodox Church, Holy Trinity, at the corner of Fishburne and St. Philip Streets. By 1923 the church included the city's first Greek school.

In 1936 the community realized the need for a center of Greek culture and social activity. Their plans for what became the Hellenic Community Center called for its erection next to the parish house on St. Philip Street. In 1940 it was decided that the property at 30 Race Street would be more suitable. Archbishop Athenagoras, primate of the Greek Orthodox Church of South and North America, was present at the elaborate dedication ceremony.

By 1940 more than 180 families of Greek descent were living in Charleston. Throughout World War II plans were formulated for a new church building. Finally, in 1953, the present structure was completed. Holy Trinity Greek Orthodox Church in Charleston is the first church in the United States built in the authentic Byzantine style of architecture with the dome over the nave. The design for the church was recommended by Archbishop Athenagoras and approved by His Eminence, Archbishop Michael. The architect was Harold Tatum of Charleston.

Byzantine architecture has as its model the Hagia Sophia, the Church of the Holy Wisdom of God, built in the fourth century by Emperor Justinian of the Byzantine Empire. It features vaults and arches, domes, patterns of low relief, mosaics, and rich, sumptuous colors.

Accordingly, the central dome of Holy Trinity rises 50 feet and contains thirteen windows that depict the life of Christ from the Annunciation to the Ascension. There are six chandeliers 4 feet in diameter, copies of those in Hagia Sophia, which are 18 feet in diameter. The church is divided into the narthex, where tradition says the learners stand; the nave, where believers stand; the solea, where the seven sacraments take place; and the sanctuary, which represents heaven and houses the Eucharist.

The icons in the church were made in Greece by the world famous iconographer Fotis Kondoglou. In 1982 this iconography was expanded by John Terzis of Chicago, an associate of Kondoglou, who painted *The Hospitality of Abraham and Sarah* above the holy altar.

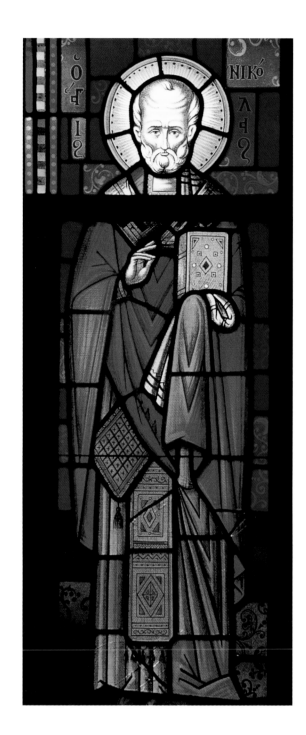

One of Holy Trinity's icons

Afterword

In its earliest years the Preservation Society of Charleston worked with other organizations to foster the preservation of a number of important dwellings in Charleston. We advocated Charleston's 1931 preservation zoning ordinance, America's first such ordinance and the model for others around the world. Since that time the Society has participated in a variety of preservation projects, such as the 1967 restoration of the famous Henry Erben Tracker organ in the Huguenot Church.

Since Hurricane Hugo in 1989, Charleston has faced a multiplying number of preservation issues, mainly concerned with the effort to maintain its residential base and the problems that come with increased traffic into the city. We still walk the thin line between saving a unique American city for future generations while simultaneously keeping the city alive and economically viable.

The Preservation Society believes that sensible preservation is good for progress. As the recognition of the value of preservation increases, we hope that stewardship of our sacred places will continue to grow. An address given by the Reverend A. Coile Estes of First (Scots) Presbyterian Church at a conference on church preservation in 1991 speaks eloquently for Charleston's religious heritage, and for a city where community has long been synonymous with stewardship.

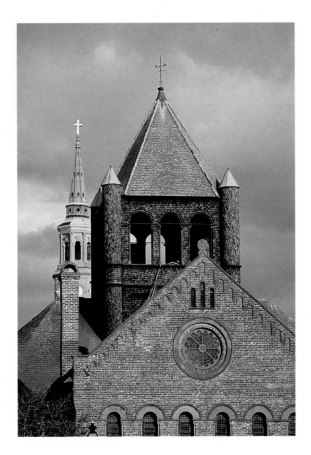

Circular Congregarional Church and in the background, the steeple of St. Philip's Episcopal Church

An Address Given at *A Legacy of Faith: Conference on the Preservation of Sacred Places,*
Sponsored by Partners for Sacred Places, Historic Augusta, 1991
by the Reverend A. Coile Estes,
First (Scots) Presbyterian Church, Charleston

"The duration of a family story is five generations. This story has been passed from my grandmother's grandmother unto me." So said the solo performer in a Piccolo Spoleto production of several years past. To know who you are, you have to tell the stories of your family. And tell them she did. For an hour and a half she traced the births, the deaths, the marriages, the hardships and the triumphs of her family. o know who you are, you have to tell the stories of your family. Those of us who are preservationists and those of us in the church are in the business of telling stories as well. Preservationists tell the stories of buildings and houses and the people who inhabited them in the past. We in the church tell stories of our family of faith, from biblical stories to the stories of people who built our churches.

The problem is that when we tell our stories we don't speak the same language. Preservationists talk about demolition by neglect and adaptive use (or is it reuse?), while we in the church use some rather strange words of our own, words like *sanctification, justification,* and that old Presbyterian favorite, *predestination.*

There are two languages that lie at the heart of what we do. They are the language of stewardship and the language of community. We need to understand both in order to work together.

We need to learn the language of stewardship. It is important for us to see ourselves not as owners but as stewards of the gifts God has given us. It is poor stewardship not to recycle; recycling applies to buildings as well as to newspapers and aluminum cans. Our resources are finite; we are called to use them carefully and responsibly.

Historic buildings are a legacy from our ancestors in the faith. Their stewardship has enabled us to inherit the gift of a historic building.

Our stewardship, our care, and our use of these buildings will determine whether or not we will pass this legacy on to another generation.

But we are not just stewards of the buildings. We are also stewards of the intangible gifts of the people who have gone before us. The work of their hands and their God-given talents are bequeathed to us in historic houses of worship which provide physical evidence that we are part of the chain of God's people who have worshiped and served in a particular place.

Good stewardship demonstrates itself in an ongoing maintenance program, an endeavor that makes good use of our money and our time. It tells the world that we care about our place of worship and that we are an active congregation rather than some relic from another time falling into disrepair. Ongoing maintenance proclaims that we are committed to continuing our worship and our service in that particular place. No matter what the size, a well-maintained historic church or synagogue with an active program attracts visitors, can lead to an increase in membership, and becomes a place where people feel fortunate to be able to worship.

So we have to learn the language of stewardship. And we have to learn the language of community. A church is a place to build community. A historic church is a place to augment the community that already exists.

The issue is not buildings versus people. The issue is buildings used by people to build a community. We have long lived in a world that has assumed that anything contemporary is good. Ours is a society that, according to one author, "encourages us to cut free from the past, define our own selves, and choose the groups with which to identify." Unfortunately, that mindset has led to many isolated individuals in desperate need of community. Part of building community is to be in touch with the past, to hear the stories of those who have gone before us and to let them shape who we are.

Historic churches and temples provide that kind of community of memory. To worship in a historic building puts us physically in touch with the past, not only because we hear the stories of our ancestors in the faith but also because we touch the work of their hands. These tangible signs of a rich heritage give us a sense that we are part of something greater than ourselves. The historic building becomes part of the foundation of our identity as a community. What a gift this historic sense of community has to offer, not only to our congregations, but to those visitors and newcomers who are searching for community in this modern world.

Now for the practical side. Church renovations are difficult because so many people are involved. If you have ever participated in a church building or renovation program, you know what I mean. There is a group that wants to do things as cheaply as possible: "Oh, we don't need to pay

for that. My cousin Jim will do it for free." There is a group that wants to do it as quickly as possible: "It will take six months to find slate to match the roof. Let's just put a regular roof up there." There is a group that is not interested in the practice of preventive maintenance: "Just patch the crack and paint over it. That's good enough." There may even be a group that thinks you should pack up and move to a new church in the suburbs.

So clergy and lay leaders who care about preservation have to take the lead in making sure that our congregations know how to restore a historic church. The key to restoring and maintaining a historic church is to have expert advice in developing a plan and expert advice on raising the money.

Begin by contacting a preservation group for guidance, expertise, and advice. It may be a local preservation group like the Preservation Society of Charleston, Historic Charleston Foundation, or the City of Charleston's Board of Architectural Review, or a private preservation consulting group. It may be a state group like the

Dates of Organization
and Extant Church Structures

CONGREGATION	DATE ORGANIZED	PRESENT STRUCTURE
St. Philip's Episcopal Church	1680	1838
Independent Church of Charleston		
(Circular Congregational Church)	c. 1681	1891
French Huguenot Church	1681	1845
Quaker (Quaker Meeting House)	c. 1682	
First Baptist Church	1686	1822
Pompion Hill Chapel	1703	1765
St. Thomas and St. Denis Episcopal Church	1706	1819
Christ Episcopal Church, Mount Pleasant	1706	1768
St. James Santee Parish Church	1706	1768
Old St. Andrew's Episcopal Church	c. 1706	1723
*Biggin Church Ruins, Berkeley County	1706	
St. James Goose Creek Episcopal Church	1707	c. 1713
Johns Island Presbyterian Church	1710	1719
Presbyterian Church on Edisto Island	1710	1834
St. John's Episcopal Church, Berkeley		
(Strawberry Chapel)	c. 1725	c. 1725
First (Scots) Presbyterian Church	1731	1814
St. John's Lutheran Church	c. 1742	1818
Kahal Kadosh Beth Elohim	1749	1840
St. Michael's Episcopal Church	1751	1761
Sheldon Chapel Ruins, Near Gardens Corner	1753	1779
Trinity Episcopal Church, Edisto Island	1774	1880
St. Mary's Catholic Church	c. 1789	1839
Trinity United Methodist Church	1791	1850
Emanuel A.M.E. Church	c. 1791	1891
Bethel United Methodist Church	1797	1853
St. James United Methodist Church	1797	1858
Second Presbyterian Church	1809	1811
Cathedral of St. Luke and St. Paul	1810	1816
*Edisto Island Baptist Church	1812	c. 1818
Unitarian Church	1817	1787
Cathedral of St. John the Baptist	1821	1907
St. Stephen's Episcopal Church	1822	1836
*Church of the Redeemer (Seamen's Chapel)	1823	1916
Mount Pleasant Presbyterian Church	1827	1847
St. Paul's Episcopal Church, Summerville	1830	1857

*Area church organized before 1900 not covered in this book

CONGREGATION	DATE ORGANIZED	PRESENT STRUCTURE
*Old Hibben Methodist Church, Mount Pleasant		
(Now Seventh Day Adventist Church)	c. 1830	1901
Christ St. Paul's Church, Adams Run	1834	1887
St. Andrew's Episcopal Church, Mount Pleasant	1835	1857
*Christ Church Ruin, Wilton Bluff	1836	1836
St. Patrick's Catholic Church	1837	1887
Grace Chapel, Rockville, Wadmalaw Island	1840	1884
St. Matthew's Lutheran Church	1840	1872
*Stono Baptist Church, Ravenel	1842	c. 1855
*Summerall Chapel, The Citadel	1842	1937
Stella Maris, Sullivan's Island	1845	1873
Grace Episcopal Church	1846	1848
Church of the Holy Communion	1848	1855
Rockville Presbyterian Church	1850	1850
Moving Star Hall, Johns Island	unknown	c. 1913
Brith Sholom Beth Israel	1854	1945
Citadel Square Baptist Church	1854	1856
Summerville Presbyterian Church	1859	1895
*St. Joseph's Catholic Church		
(Now St. John's Reformed Episcopal Church)	1861	1850
Centenary United Methodist Church	c. 1862	1842
*Mount Hebron Presbyterian Church, Johns Island	1865	c. 1865
St. Mark's Episcopal Church	1865	1878
St. Andrew's Lutheran Church	1866	1834
*St. Peter's Catholic Church	1866	1847
Morris Brown A.M.E. Church	1867	1875
*Salem Missionary Baptist Church	1867	1912
*Wallingford Presbyterian Church	1867	1867
*Trinity A.M.E. Church	1870	1907
*Bethel A.M.E. Church, McClellanville	1872	1891
*New Wappetaw Presbyterian Church	1872	1875
*Promised Land Reformed Episcopal, Johns Island	c. 1873	c. 1875
*Wesley Methodist Church, Lincolnville	c. 1874	1887
*Israel Reformed Episcopal Church	c. 1875	1884
Holy Trinity Reformed Episcopal Church	1875	1880
New Tabernacle Fourth Baptist Church	1875	1862
St. Johannes Lutheran Church	1878	1842
Old Bethel United Methodist Church	1880	1797
St. Paul's Evangelical Lutheran Church, Mount Pleasant	1881	1884
Mt. Zion A.M.E. Church	1882	1847
*St. Barnabas Lutheran Church	1883	1921
St. Stephen's Reformed Episcopal Church,		
Summerville	1885	c. 1885
*Memorial Baptist Church	1886	1886
St. James Santee Chapel, McClellanville	1890	1890
Central Baptist Church	1891	1891
*St. Luke's Lutheran Church, Summerville	1892	1893
*Central Reformed Methodist Episcopal	1897	1897
St. John's Reformed Episcopal Church	1906	1850
Holy Trinity Greek Orthodox Church	1909	1953
Bishop Pengelley Memorial Chapel, Summerville	1945	1891
St. Luke's Chapel, Medical University of South Carolina	1966	1883

Bibliography

Armstrong, Richard S. *The Preservation of Churches, Synagogues and Other Religious Structures.* Information Series no. 17. Washington, D.C.: National Trust for Historic Preservation, 1978.

Baird, Charles W. *Huguenot Emigration to America.* Baltimore: Regional Publishing, 1966.

Baker, Robert A., and Craven, Paul, Jr. *Adventure in Faith: The First 300 Years of First Baptist Church, Charleston, S.C.* Nashville: Broadman Press, 1982.

Batson, Annie Jenkins. *Rockville Presbyterian Church on Wadmalaw Island S.C.: The Early 1770s–1975.* Charleston: Walker, Evans & Cogswell, July 1976.

Beesley, Charles Norbury. *Beesley Illustrated Guide to St. Michael's Church.* Charleston: Walker, Evans & Cogswell, 1898.

Bernheim, G. D. *History of the German Settlements and of the Lutheran Church in North and South Carolina.* Philadelphia: Lutheran Book Store, 1872.

Betts, Albert Deems. *History of South Carolina Methodism.* Columbia, S.C.: Advocate Press, 1952.

Bogne, D., and Bennet, J. *History of Dissenters, from the Revolution in 1688 to 1808.* London, 1808.

Boles, John B. *The Great Revival, 1787–1805: The Origins of the Southern Evangelical Mind.* Lexington: University of Kentucky Press, 1972.

Bolton, S. Charles. *Southern Anglicanism: the Church of England in Colonial South Carolina.* Westport, Conn.: Greenwood Press, 1982.

Breibart, Solomon. "The Synagogues of Kahal Kadosh Beth Elohim of Charleston, South Carolina," *South Carolina Historical Magazine* 80, no. 3 (July 1989): 215–235.

Bridenbaugh, Carl. *Myths and Realities: Societies of the Colonial South.* New York: Atheneum, 1967.

Brinsfield, John Wesley. *Religion and Politics in Colonial South Carolina.* Greenville: Southern Historical Press, 1983.

Burton, E. Milby. *The Siege of Charleston, 1861–1865.* Columbia: University of South Carolina Press, 1970.

Calhoon, Robert McCluer. *Evangelicals and Conservatives in the Early South.* Columbia: University of South Carolina Press, 1988.

Cheshire, Bishop J. B. *The Church in the Confederate States.* Charleston: Dalcho Historical Society of the Diocese of South Carolina, 1912.

Chreitzberg, A. M. *Early Methodism in the Carolinas.* Nashville: Publishing House of the Methodist Episcopal Church South, 1897.

Clute, Robert F. *The Annals and Parish Register of St. Thomas and St. Denis Parish in South Carolina from 1680–1884.* Charleston: Walker, Evans & Cogswell, 1884.

Crevecoeur, J. Hector St. John de. *Letters from an American Farmer.* New York: Dutton, 1957.

Dalcho, Frederick. *An Historical Account of the Protestant Episcopal Church in South Carolina.* Charleston: A. E. Miller, 1820.

Davis, Richard Beale. *Intellectual Life in the Colonial South, 1585–1763.* Knoxville: University of Tennessee Press, 1978.

Dorsey, Stephen Palmer. *Early English Churches in America, 1607–1807.* New York: Oxford University Press, 1952.

Edwards, George N. *A History of the Independent or Congregational Church of Charleston, South Carolina* Boston: Pilgrim Press, 1947.

Elzas, Barnett A. *The Jews of South Carolina from the Earliest Times to the Present Day.* Philadelphia: J. B. Lippincott Company, 1905.

Farmer, James Oscar. *The Metaphysical Confederacy: James Henley Thornwell and the Synthesis of Southern Values.* Macon, Ga.: Mercer University Press, 1896.

Fraser, Antonia. *Royal Charles: Charles II and the Restoration.* New York: Knopf, 1980.

Fraser, Walter J. *Charleston! Charleston! The History of a Southern City.* Columbia: University of South Carolina Press, 1989.

Gilman, Samuel. *The Old and the New; or Discourses and Proceedings at the Dedication of the Re-modelled Unitarian Church in Charleston.* Charleston: Samuel G. Courtenay, 1854.

Goen, C. C. *Broken Churches, Broken Nation: Denominational Schism and the Coming of the American Civil War.* Macon, Ga.: Mercer University Press, 1985.

Grant, Henry Martyn. *Circular Church, Charleston, S.C.* N.P., 1890.

Guy, Yvette Richardson. *A History of Trinity United Methodist Church, from Dissension to Unity.* Charleston: Trinity United Methodist Church, 1991.

Heitzler, Michael. *Historic Goose Creek, South Carolina 1670–1980.* Greenville: Southern Historical Press, Inc., 1982.

Hennessy, Florence Marie. *In the Beginning . . . St. Mary's Church, Charleston, S.C. 1789–1989.* Charleston: St. Mary's Church, 1989.

Hill, Samuel S. *Encyclopedia of Religion in the South.* Macon, Ga.: Mercer University Press, 1984.

Hirsch, Arthur Henry. *The Huguenots of Colonial South Carolina.* Durham: Duke University Press, 1928.

Holifield, E. Brooks. *The Gentlemen Theologians: American Theology in Southern Culture, 1795–1860.* Durham: Duke University Press, 1928.

Howe, Christopher G. and McCrady, Edward, et al. *Historic St. Philip's Episcopal Church.* Charleston: St. Philip's Church Mice, 1981.

Howe, George. *History of the Presbyterian Church in South Carolina.* Columbia: Duffie and Chapman, 1870.

Huff, Archie Vernon, Jr. *A History of South Carolina United Methodism*. Columbia: South Carolina Conference of the United Methodist Church, 1984.

Kenner, H. C. *Historical Records of Trinity Episcopal Church, Edisto Island*. Edisto: Trinity Episcopal Church, 1975.

Larisey, Mary Maxine. *The Unitarian Church in Charleston, S.C.: A History*. Charleston: The Women's Alliance of the Unitarian Church in Charleston, 1967.

Lawton, Samuel Miller. "Abstract of the Religious Life of South Carolina Coastal and Sea Island Negroes," *Contributions to Education* (Nashville). No. 242, 1939, pp. 2–3.

Leland, Isabella G. *Charleston: Crossroads of History*. Woodland Hills, Cal.: Charleston Trident Chamber of Commerce/Windson Publications, 1980.

Lilly, Edward Guerrant. *Beyond the Burning Bush: First (Scots) Presbyterian Church*. Columbia: The R. L. Bryan Company, 1986.

Lilly, Edward Guerrant. *Historic Churches of Charleston, South Carolina*. Charleston: Legerton and Company, 1966.

Liscombe, Rhodie Windsor. *The Church Architecture of Robert Mills*. Easley, S.C.: Southern Historical Press, 1985.

Marsh, Blanche. *Robert Mills: Architect in South Carolina*. Columbia: The R. L. Bryan Company, 1970.

Marty, Martin E. *Righteous Empire: The Protestant Experience in America*. New York: Dial Press, 1970.

Mathews, Donald G. *Religion in the Old South*. Chicago: University of Chicago Press, 1977.

McCrady, Edward. *The History of South Carolina under the Proprietary Government, 1670–1719*. New York: Russell and Russell, 1969.

Molloy, Robert. *Charleston: A Gracious Heritage*. New York: D. Appleton-Century Company, 1947.

Mortimer, Roger. *Aspects of the Western Religious Heritage: A Catalogue to an Exhibition in Commemoration of that Ecumenical Year*. Columbia: University of South Carolina Press, 1987.

O'Brien, Michael and Moltke-Hansen, David. *Intellectual Life in Antebellum Charleston*. Knoxville: University of Tennessee Press, 1986.

Preservation Consultants. *Charleston Countywide Survey of Historic Sites*. South Carolina Department of Archives and History. State Preservation Office Files. South Carolina Statewide Survey Files. National Register of Historic Places Files. Draft, 1992.

Quattlebaum, Alberta Lachicotte and Pinckney, Elise. *A Guide to St. Michael's Church, Charleston*. Charleston: St. Michael's Vestry, 1979.

Ramsay, David. *History of the Congregational Independent Church of Charleston, S.C.* Philadelphia, 1815.

Ravenel, Beatrice St. Julien. *Architects of Charleston*. Charleston: Carolina Art Association, 1945; Columbia: University of South Carolina Press 1992.

Ravenel, Mrs. St. Julien. *Charleston: The Place and the People*. New York: Macmillan, 1906.

Rhett, Robert Goodwin. *Charleston: An Epic of Carolina*. Richmond, 1940.

Rogers, George C., Jr. *Charleston in the Age of the Pinckneys*. Norman: University of Oklahoma Press, 1969; Columbia: University of South Carolina Press, 1980.

Rogers, George C., Jr. *Church and State in Eighteenth Century South Carolina*. Charleston: Dalcho Historical Society, 1959.

Rosen, Robert. *A Short History of Charleston*. San Francisco: Lexikos, 1982.

Severens, Kenneth. *Charleston: Antebellum Architecture and Civic Destiny*. Knoxville: University of Tennessee Press, 1988.

Shipp, Albert M. *History of Methodism in South Carolina*. Nashville: Southern Methodist Publishing House, 1883.

Simons, Albert and Lapham, Samuel, Jr. *The Early Architecture of Charleston*. Columbia: University of South Carolina Press, 1927 and 1970.

Specifications of the Materials and Work for the New German Lutheran Church [St. Matthew's]. Charleston: Joseph Walker, 1867.

Steedman, Marguerite Couturier. *A Short History of the French Protestant Church of Charleston, South Carolina*. Charleston: Nelson's Southern Printing, 1970.

Stockton, Robert and Preservation Consultants. *Historic Resources of Berkeley County, South Carolina*. Berkeley County: Berkeley County Historical Society, 1990.

Stokes, Durwood T. "The Baptist and Methodist Clergy in South Carolina," *South Carolina Historical Magazine*. LXXIII (1972), p. 89.

Stoney, Samuel Gaillard. *Colonial Church Architecture in South Carolina*. Charleston: The Dalcho Historical Society, 1954.

Stoney, Samuel Gaillard. *Plantations of the Carolina Lowcountry*. Charleston: Carolina Art Association, 1938; Dover, 1989.

Stoney, Samuel Gaillard. *This is Charleston: A Survey of the Architectural Heritage of a Unique American City*. Charleston: Carolina Art Association, 1944.

Thomas, Albert Sidney. *The Episcopal Church of Edisto Island: Trinity, Edisto, and the First Confirmations in the Diocese of South Carolina*. Charleston: The Dalcho Historical Society, 1953.

Thomas, Albert Sidney. *A Historical Account of the Protestant Episcopal Church in South Carolina 1820–1957*. Columbia: The R. L. Bryan Company, 1959.

Thompson, Ernest Trice. *Presbyterians in the South*. Richmond: John Knox Press, 1963.

Tompkins, George Johnson, III. *The Ashes of Our Fathers, the Temples of Our God: An Architectural History of Saint Andrew's Parish Church, Charleston, S.C. With Proposals for Restoration and a Columbarium*. Dissertation, University of the South, Sewanee, Tennessee.

Wallace, David Duncan. *The Historical Background of Religion in South Carolina*. Charleston: The Dalcho Historical Society, 1916.

Whitelaw, Robert N. S. and Levkoff, Alice F. *Charleston, Come Hell or High Water*. Columbia: The R. L. Bryan Company, 1975.

Williams, George W. *St. Michael's, Charleston, 1751–1951*. Columbia: University of South Carolina Press, 1951.

Wilson, Charles. *Religion in the South: Essays*. Jackson: University of Mississippi Press, 1985.

Wood, Peter H. *Black Majority: Negroes in Colonial South Carolina from 1670 through the Stono Rebellion*. New York: Knopf, 1974.

Woodward, C. Vann. *The Burden of Southern History*. New York: Vintage Books, 1960. [Baton Rouge: Louisiana State University Press, 1960.]

Index